womenconnected

womenconnected

PAM BARTLETT

A Session-by-Session Coaching Guide for Women's Groups

WOMEN CONNECTED

Published by

Glenmoore Press

P.O. Box 68

Greenbank, Washington 98253

1-800-693-4919

FIRST EDITION

Cover and Interior Design by Shannon McCafferty

Cover Illustration by Obadinah Heavner

Library of Congress Cataloging-in-Publication Data

Bartlett, Pamela

Women Connected: a session-by-session coaching guide for women's groups /by Pamela Bartlett.

Library of Congress Control Number 2006920675

ISBN-10: 0-9776656-0-7

ISBN-13: 978-0-9776656-0-0

1. Women's Issues 2. Coaching 3. Leadership

4. Group Facilitation 5. Communication

I. Title: Women Connected. II. Title

0 9 8 7 6 5 4 3 2 1

The poem "Stars" is reprinted with kind permission of the publisher. From *Turning to One Another: Simple Conversations to Restore Hope to the Future*, copyright© 2002 by Margaret J. Wheatley, Berrett-Koehler Publishers, Inc., San Francisco, CA. All rights reserved. www.bkconnection.com

This book is lovingly dedicated to all women everywhere who long for deeper connections and a new world of possibilities.

Contents

Introduction

ago. My current women's group has been together nine years, and there seems to be no end in sight! The women in this group (Anne, Carol, Cheryl, Debbie, Linda, Peggy, Stella, and Victoria) listen to my stories, nudge me past obstacles that seem insurmountable, and believe that I can achieve my ever-expanding dreams. They are my reality checkers when I get out of sync, and with honest feedback and loving support they have given me one of the most precious gifts—their time.

Over 15 years ago I began to facilitate women's groups, and have continued to do so to this day. The first group was named Women Connected, a simple name that seemed to capture the essence of what we all most wanted from our sessions together—a time to connect, a place to belong. This book is my attempt to share what I've learned over the years about how women connect. I wanted to offer to other women the nuts-and-bolts techniques that would make it easy to start their own Women Connected groups.

HOW TO USE THIS BOOK

I'll begin with a brief description of the parts of a typical Women Connected session. I have found over the years that this design works extremely well for building a group on a solid foundation. Then I'll lead you through 11 sessions that I promise will change your life and the lives of the women you choose to include in your circle. You may want to begin by reading through Chapter 1 "An Evening of Exploration" and Chapter 2 "New Beginnings" to help in planning your first few gatherings. Of course, you may use any of the group session activities that follow just as they are given, but I hope you'll also feel free to add to them in your own way.

Each Women Connected chapter provides tools, group resources, practical suggestions, and a script, all in a standardized format, so you can host a successful group session with confidence. Every chapter is titled with the name of the topic to be covered, starting with a detailed description of why the topic is important and what you and group members can expect to gain by participating in the session. Next you'll find a schedule with the suggested length of time to allot for each activity. After this big-picture view, you'll find a complete script for the host of the session. The script leads you through the activities that make Women Connected groups successful in producing long-lasting results.

At the end of every chapter, you'll find thoughts to assist you in summarizing the session and weaving it into the next one, as well as supporting handouts and preparation material for the following session. This preparation material is called the Session Accelerator, and it's designed to maximize the effectiveness of the time you spend together and help you get a head start on the next topic. I strongly suggest that your group commit to completing the Session Accelerator prior to each meeting. You'll also find a list of resources at the back of the book, including a reading list and helpful troubleshooting tips.

So get ready! You're about to give yourself a wonderful gift—the gift of creating your own Women Connected group. Just imagine how your life might look next year if you got all the support you needed, if you had the kind of regular, built-in accountability that a group of committed listeners provides. As my friend Victoria says, "How good can you stand it?" I'm living proof of the power of women joining together in intentional conversations, supporting each other's goals, and expecting the best of one another. What have you got to lose? What might you gain? Even if you are absolutely satisfied with your current situation, how much better might it be if you gave yourself the gift of connection with other women? I invite you to find out just how good you can stand it. You deserve it, and so do your friends. And—because every fairytale ending needs a memorable beginning—let's begin!

There is a hidden seed of greater wholeness in everyone and everything.

□ RACHEL NAOMI REMEN

Getting Started

I believe we can change the world
if we start listening to one another again.

□ MARGARET J. WHEATLEY

You might be asking yourself, "Now what do I do?" Well, you might simply begin by saying to a couple of friends, "I want to start a women's group that will inspire us to bring out the best in one another, and support us in living our lives to our fullest. I found a book that gives step-by-step instructions for doing it successfully. I'd like to get several of us together to talk about it. Would you be interested? Who else do you know who might be willing to explore doing a group with us?"

You might also say, "I'm hosting an Evening of Exploration to talk about the possibility of setting up a Women Connected group. We'll check out the topics, and see who would like to try out the Women Connected process for two or three sessions to see if it works. The book shows how to fine-tune as we go along, to address each group member's needs. There is a mid-course evaluation we can use to insure that we continue to create value from our time together. We've got nothing to lose, and we could learn some new things about ourselves and one another. What do you think? I know a couple of women who might be interested. Do you know anyone?"

I encourage you not to try to convince your friends that a Women Connected group would be "good for them." It's best not to get in the position of trying to talk someone into the group. It's been my experience that the best groups are made up of women who really want to move forward in their lives and who are fully committed to the group process.

Just let your friends know that this first evening involves no pressure: "It will be fun and relaxing. We'll check out the Women Connected process, and then see where we'd like to go from there."

11

WHAT IT IS AND WHAT IT ISN'T

The purpose of Women Connected is to create a safe place where deep listening, acceptance of individual differences, and compassion are the norm. Women Connected is a place to show up as you are; to be seen, heard, and understood. It's a place where honesty and openness are practiced and where being vulnerable is how we connect with one another. It's a place where growth takes place through creative activities and intentional conversations. It's a group where we can reflect on what matters most to us and be inspired by the greatness of others—a place to share what's in our hearts and minds. Women Connected builds closer friendships and empowers women to live into their dreams.

Women Connected is not a place to gossip; to badmouth husbands, partners, or friends. It is designed to create intentional, forward-moving conversations rather than the typical social conversations that take place in our everyday lives. It's not therapy; you are not charged or given permission to fix people or to give unsolicited advice. It's designed to support deep conversations and focused listening in a judgment-free environment. Your task is to show up, be present, and bring your real self forward. You do not need to pretend to be someone else or show up always looking perfect. The more vulnerable you can be, the better—it will accelerate your growth and connection with your group. I have a sign in my office that reads "Change is good—you go first." I encourage you to go first. After all, who better than you to get the ball rolling!

WHO TO INVITE

Invite women you trust, the ones with whom you can share thoughts, feelings, and dreams, knowing that they'll keep your confidences. Invite interesting women who are curious about life and are willing to share their honest thoughts and feelings. Invite women who are open to change, who welcome looking at things in fresh, new ways—women who are flexible and willing to learn and grow.

HOW MANY WOMEN?

If you want six to eight women in your group, I suggest inviting 10 women to the Evening of Exploration. It's been my experience that the ideal Women Connected group has at least six women, but no more than eight. The more women, the less air time is available to each group member. You want a group that's small enough to create intimacy; not one so large that some women feel lost in a crowd or feel that there's not enough time for them to have their needs met.

TIME COMMITMENT

The issue of time will often arise right away. A Women Connected group does require a significant time commitment. Each session is designed to last $2\frac{1}{2}$ hours, and there are 11 sessions for those who want to participate in the entire program. The time you spend with your group is your time, and you are worth every minute. By spending intentional time with other women, you'll develop a greater capacity for enjoying your connections and accomplishments. This process creates lifelong friendships and deepens all your relationships.

Some groups choose to spend more time on each topic than is suggested, and therefore may spend two sessions exploring a single chapter. The session leader (Group

Guide) will need approximately 30 minutes of preparation time. (I recommend that groups rotate the Group Guide position from one session to the next.) Preparation includes reading over the chapter and preparing snacks for the break time. Prior to each session, the Group Guide will prepare enough handouts for each member's use by going to www.WomenConnected.com and downloading the handouts. Note: See "Group Guide Checklist—Everything You Need to Know and More!" in the Resources section at the back of this book. Here you will find helpful information that supports a successful Group Guide experience.

Women Connected Structure

This section contains a descriptive list of the recurring elements in each Women Connected session.

GROUP GUIDE

The role of the Group Guide is just that: to guide the flow of the session. It's useful at the beginning of each session for the Group Guide to remind members that because one of the her responsibilities is to keep the flow of the session moving along, she will appreciate everyone's support in keeping conversations intentional rather than social. It is best if group members share this role,

taking turns so each member has an opportunity to experience being the Group Guide for at least one session.

POEM

A poem is selected ahead of time by the Group Guide. It is read at the beginning of each session to set the tone and provide a time to settle in, quiet the mind, and connect the group. You will find a large selection of poetry books in the Resources section at the back of this book.

CHECK-IN

This time is scheduled at the beginning of each session to connect with the group. Group members share updates on their commitments, challenges, and accomplishments. Questions for Check-In might include:

☐ What results are showing up in my life that I like?

☐ What results are showing up that I don't like?

☐ What have been my lessons this month?

After each woman completes her Check-In, she lights a candle and states her intention for the session.

FOCUS OF THE SESSION

Each session will focus on a specific topic that accelerates personal growth and supports movement toward a clearly defined vision.

WISDOM BLAST

This is a process that is occasionally used when there is time left in the session. It is designed to access the group's collective wisdom. Each woman has the option to bring an issue, challenge, or dilemma before the group. For three minutes the group generates as many ideas as possible to help address the issue. This is the only time when giving advice is encouraged. The advice is captured by a scribe, and the recipient of the group's wisdom reports the results of the Wisdom Blast by e-mail or phone, or at the next Check-In.

CAPTURING WHAT MATTERS MOST TO ME

The learnings, insights, and memories gained at each session are documented in a personal journal or the specially designed handout at the end of each chapter. This process helps to refocus on what was covered during the session and tracks the personal growth of each individual.

MY COMMITMENTS

During each session time is set aside to write commitments aligned with each woman's purpose and clearly defined vision for the year. Clarifying each woman's purpose and vision will take place in sessions that are included in the Women Connected program.

GROWTH BUDDIES

At the end of every session, each woman is assigned one person who will be her Growth Buddy until the next session. Growth Buddies support each other in honoring their commitments, act as sounding boards when necessary, and cheer each other on between sessions.

CLOSING CIRCLE

At the end of every Women Connected session, there is a formal completion ceremony. The women in the group stand up and together form a circle, the universal symbol of unity and wholeness. Since ancient times people have gathered in circles to share stories, provide support, and gain understanding of the common good. This is a special time of closure for the group. In the Closing Circle, each woman shares a word or brief thought that expresses what she learned or how she was affected by the session. After she shares her experience, she extinguishes her candle and the session is complete.

PLANNING THE NEXT SESSION

After the Closing Circle the arrangements for the next session are discussed. A decision is made on the next session date, who the Group Guide will be, and the location. Growth Buddies are assigned to work with one another between sessions during this time. The Session Accelerator (the preparation work for the next session) is distributed.

So there you have it . . . all the information needed to begin the process of hosting your first Women Connected gathering. If you have any questions or concerns, I encourage you to read the first several chapters of the book. You'll discover that everything you need to host a successful session is included in each chapter. It takes courage to try out new things, and I want to commend you for stepping into a new adventure! I know that you'll never regret the decision, and it is a remarkable gift that you are extending to other women. You're embarking on a truly life-changing journey of self-discovery and intentional conversations that will help you turn your dreams into reality.

An Evening of

Exploration

When nothing is sure, everything is possible.

□ MARGARET DRABBLE

This may be the first time you've ever considered starting a women's group. If that is the case, it might be a good idea to host the Evening of Exploration with one other friend as your cohost—someone who's as committed as yourself. You've bought the book, you've glanced through the chapters, and you've read enough to know that a Women Connected group is something you want to do for yourselves. You don't have to do this alone; this process is all about women connecting with women, after all!

An Evening of Exploration is a great opportunity for you and the women you've invited to get a taste of the Women Connected process. It's a brief session but an important time because you'll all be deciding whether you want to continue together to do deeper exploration in this way. I encourage you to consider that you might host several such evenings, to be certain you are bringing together women who will truly support one another in living into their best selves and their highest possibilities. So don't be discouraged if you call together several women and some of them don't feel like going forward in a Women Connected group. I've had Evenings of Exploration that didn't result in enough interest to warrant creating a group, and I've hosted gatherings when everyone left feeling joyful and enthusiastic about going forward.

As the initiator of this evening, your intention must be absolutely clear. In other words, you need to be firmly committed to moving forward with Women Connected before you begin. However you don't have to know who you'll be going on this journey with, or exactly how it will look. Finding that out, arriving at a sense of commitment to working with a particular group is what this evening is all about!

If you sense any hesitancy from someone, listen to it. In that case, rather than attempting to convince her that it'll be fun to do this together (even though that may be true), it's best to take her reluctance seriously and allow her to decline gracefully. Every woman who joins the Women Connected group will need to have a high level of commitment to being fully involved that goes beyond attending a social gathering. Bailing out later is not an option! Participating in Women Connected is a process that requires each woman's willingness to go through the entire set of sessions together, going deeper into what matters most to her. For this reason, while you're still testing the waters, it's best to be picky. Don't push to make it work if, on a gut level, you feel some hesitation. In my experience it's rare when every single woman who shows up for the Evening of Exploration feels inspired to go forward with Women Connected. If at the close of the evening, however, you have a sense that these women could help each other go further into discovering their best selves, then go for it!

Remember that the ideal group size is between six and eight women. If you've invited 10 women to the Evening of Exploration and six to eight want to go forward, you're ready to begin. If at the close of the evening there are four or five women interested in creating a group, you might host another evening to provide the opportunity to three or four additional women who can fully commit to Women Connected. If you decide to hold another Evening of Exploration, I suggest that the women who have already decided to commit to a Women Connected group attend the session. This will give the new invitees a chance to see if there is a fit for them with the group. It will also give those of you who have decided to move forward with Women Committed a chance to share why you are ready to commit.

Another option is to simply ask each of the interested women to help you invite and educate their friends about the intention of this group, and in that way fill the group. At the same time, if five of you have a strong inspiration to go forward and you don't feel you need additional members to make it work, honor your commitment to one another and go ahead. The suggested group size is based on my experience, but it certainly isn't the only way that Women Connected can work. Each group has its own brand of wisdom, and acknowledging that is a wonderful way to begin.

Words of Wisdom

Ask people to come early. Allow at least 30 minutes before the Evening of Exploration begins for welcoming, social interaction, and late arrivals. Once everyone is settled, you can begin the activity.

When women come together, we usually enjoy caring for one another. We like feeding and entertaining our guests and providing comfort. While our enjoyment of tending and befriending one another is important, it's essential to maintain the focus of the group on intentional conversation. Remember that the purpose of the evening is to decide whether you want to become a group. This isn't the time to bring out your best gourmet cooking or to pressure yourself to create a party environment. It's good to hold the evening after the dinner hour and simply provide water and nonalcoholic beverages for the meeting time. After the Evening of Exploration session activities end, you could provide desserts and coffee or other beverages for those who can stay and socialize. Modeling this approach from the beginning will help all future Group Guides of your Women Connected sessions to do the same.

You could also host a Morning or Afternoon of Exploration; the session doesn't have to take place in the evening. The important feature is that the Exploration does not occur during a mealtime.

Bumps in the Road—With Solutions!

SOCIAL CONVERSATIONS

When women come together, our first impulse is to converse socially. It's the way we naturally connect, and it's the kind of connection with which we have the most experience. A Women Connected group, however, is a gathering with a specific purpose. In order for all the members to get the most out of their time together, it's essential for them to agree to maintain the intention of the conversation.

Solution: It's useful if the Group Guide

reminds members that one of her responsibilities is to keep the session moving along, and that she would appreciate everyone's support in keeping conversations intentional rather than social. When someone begins sharing a story or anecdote that doesn't relate directly to the topic, one of the group members may say something like: "I'm really interested in what you have to say, and I'm also noticing that we might be slipping into a social conversation. Our time is so precious here that I'd like to bring our focus back to the original topic. I'd love to hear more about this after we've completed our session."

KEEPING TRACK OF TIME

In the spirit of keeping commitments and honoring one another's time, it's important to start and end on time. This is a way that you can begin to model the type of behavior and norms that are a part of a successful Women Connected group. Arriving fashionably late is not part of the program! **Solution:** During your session, it's helpful to designate a timekeeper. For the Evening of Exploration, the cohosts can share this responsibility by taking turns setting the timer at the beginning of each timed activity.

Debbie's Story

My friend Debbie and I have always had a special connection—so much so that we can almost finish each other's sentences. Her sparkling eyes and warm way of welcoming people makes her the kind of woman everyone wants for her girlfriend. She's strong and loves adventure. Before she married her husband of 23 years she traveled around the world, and she speaks fluent Spanish and Portuguese. But aside from all that, Debbie's just fun to be with—the light in her readily flows out. A 30-year yoga student and a mother, with a graduate degree in social work, she's a recent empty nester whose youngest child just graduated from high school.

Debbie has been facilitating personal growth, therapeutic, and weight loss groups for over two decades. The thought often occurred to her that she would like to explore her life, reconnect with her purpose, and create a new vision for the next half of her life. Debbie's children were launching into adulthood and her career needed a tune-up. It was the perfect time to invite her women friends to an Evening of Exploration. Her friends invited their friends, and before she knew it nine women had agreed to attend this exploratory session. During this first evening it became clear that having the connection with other women in this setting provided what Debbie was longing for—

a support group to challenge her thinking, encourage her goals, and inspire her in meeting the challenges that she faced. By the end of the evening eight women had committed to going forward with Women Connected. Debbie felt a renewed sense of purpose and was proud that she had given herself the gift of this special evening.

It had been fun, and now she was excited about the opportunity to develop these friendships in an intentional way that facilitated their personal growth. Since that first evening, the members of Debbie's Women Connected group have forged such a strong bond that they are still meeting regularly, two years later.

The Big Picture: An Evening of Exploration

Suggested Time Frames	Activity	Purpose	Materials	Set-up
:05	Opening	Welcome; transition into Women Connected; become present	• Poem
:30	Check-In	Introductions, connections	• Candle for each woman
1:40	Session: An Evening of Exploration	Explore the Women Connected structure. This is a group that is designed to support your on-going development; you will be deciding whether this group is a match for you.	• Handout 1.1 Women Connected Benefits • Handout 1.2 Women Connected 11-Session Coaching Guide • Handout 1.3 Women Connected Structure • Handout 1.4 My Wish List
:10	Closing Circle	Opportunity to complete the session	• Standing circle • Extinguish candles
:25	Logistics for next session	Ensure Group continuity and clarity of requirements for the next session	• Designate Group Guide, time, place • Choose a Growth Buddy • Session Accelerator 2.1 A Special Object • Session Accelerator 2.2 All About Me

What Happens During
"An Evening of Exploration" Session
0:00 WELCOME: GROUP GUIDES
(5 MINUTES)

Prior to starting the group, place a candle for each woman near the location where the group will be gathered. Each woman will light a candle at the completion of her Check-In.

We'd like to thank you for coming to my home this evening to learn about Women Connected. We'll spend the next two hours exploring what Women Connected is and getting to know one another better. You can expect that your questions will get answered and that we'll have fun together. So let me explain to you what we'll be doing tonight.

We will look at:

☐ What is Women Connected?

☐ What can I expect to gain if I were to participate?

☐ What is the structure?

☐ What would be expected from me if I were to commit to Women Connected?

The Women Connected Coaching Guide is a well-tested format that produces amazing results. By following this tried-and-true map, we won't have to create our women's group from scratch. With Women Connected, we are joining with hundreds of other women

What You'll Need
- Poem
- Candle for each woman
- Digital timer
- Personal journal or notebook
- Calendar for setting next session's date
- Handout 1.1 Women Connected Benefits
- Handout 1.2 Women Connected 11-Session Coaching Guide
- Handout 1.3 Women Connected Structure
- Handout 1.4 My Wish List
- Session Accelerator 2.1 A Special Object
- Session Accelerator 2.2 All About Me

All handouts and Session Accelerators are provided as downloadable files at www.WomenConnected.com

who have successfully used this coaching group process to reclaim their lives and put their dreams in motion!

Tonight we will experience some of the key elements of Women Connected sessions. Each session starts with a poem, followed by a moment of silence, a time for checking in, and then the individual lighting of candles, which represent bringing new light into our lives.

I'd like to start by reading a poem. This is an opportunity for us to be still, settle in, and let the outside world be where it belongs . . . outside. We are inside together now; present to what is possible when women are connected.

Group Guide reads her preselected poem.
After the poem is read say:
Each Women Connected session has a Check-In component. The purpose is to reconnect with one another, to get current on commitments we've made and goals achieved. It's a time to bring ourselves fully into the session and set external distractions aside. One person speaks at a time. There are no questions or interruptions. This is not a time for giving feedback or advice. This is a time to listen deeply.

0:05 CHECK-IN/INTRODUCTIONS (30 MINUTES)

In this first Check-In, I'll ask you to introduce yourself and then answer the following question: What is happening in your life right now that might make a woman's coaching group a good place to be?

We'll spend a few minutes thinking about our responses, and then I'll go first. Each of us will have two minutes to complete her Check-In. I will set the digital timer at the beginning of each Check-In. When the two minutes is complete for my Check-In, the person on my right will go next. I'll set the timer for each person until we have completed the Check-In process.

The Group Guide goes first, in order to model the Check-In process. The key is to keep the individual's Check-In brief, no longer than two minutes. It's easy to eat up a lot of time during Check-In and it's important to keep things moving. Remember to set the digital timer for each individual's Check-In.
After Check-In is complete:
Thank you for bringing yourselves fully to the Check-In. As you can see, it's a great way to connect and be present with one another.

Remember to have each woman light a candle and state her intention for the session after she has completed her Check-In. This process will be repeated every session.

0:35 LET'S GET ACQUAINTED—ACTIVITY (18 MINUTES)

Our first activity tonight is an example of something we would do during a Women Connected coaching session. Each session has a specific focus, with activities structured to achieve specific results. The activities are interactive and highly participative. Sometimes we'll work in pairs, sometimes in small groups, and sometimes as an entire group. Tonight's activities are in keeping with part of the overall intent of Women Connected, which is getting to know one another at a deeper level. This activity provides practice in asking questions, being curious, and discovering unusual events in one another's lives.

A suggestion for this activity and those that follow: Break into groups or pairs first, and then give directions for the activity. When this is done, everyone is ready to go and will be more likely to hear the instructions. Doing this also speeds up the overall process.

Divide yourselves into two equal groups. (*Pause for a moment and wait to give instructions until everyone is settled in a group.*) Each group will designate a scribe who will also act as the reporter for the group. The scribe, or reporter, will write down your responses to the following question:

☐   What do we all have in common?

We will have five minutes to list 15 or more commonalties. Some examples of the questions you might ask of your group are: Is everyone married? Does everyone like pizza? Do we all drive a car? Have we all traveled out of the country? Be creative, ask questions of one another, and see how many things you share in common!

Group Guide sets digital timer for five minutes and participates in one of the groups.

After five minutes Group Guide says:
Scribes/reporters please tally your group's responses to the question. Which group came up with the most unanimous similarities? What was the most unusual similarity that your group has in common?

Take time to listen to the responses from the various groups. (2-3 minutes)

It's now time for the second round. We'll have eight minutes to identify 15 or more answers to the following question:
☐ How are we different from everyone in the group?

Some examples of questions you might ask of the women in your group are:
☐ What have you done that no one else has done?
☐ What makes you unique and special?

Some examples that you might offer to your group are places traveled, number of children in your family, unusual experience or adventure, favorite hobbies, etc. Select a new scribe/reporter and I'll be the timekeeper.

Group Guide sets digital timer for eight minutes. After eight minutes Group Guide says:
Time is up, scribes/reporters please tally the responses.

LET'S GET ACQUAINTED—LARGE GROUP DISCUSSION (7 MINUTES)
Group Guide leads a discussion of the activity. Suggested questions to ask the group:
- ☐ Which group came up with the most differences?
- ☐ What were some of the most unusual or unique experiences that were discovered in each group?
- ☐ What was your experience of this activity?
- ☐ What did you learn about one another?
- ☐ Was anyone surprised by what they discovered?

At the completion of this activity, Group Guide might say something like:
This group has a large and varied background of experiences, likes, and dislikes. The depth of wisdom available within this group is truly remarkable.

Women Connected is designed to make the most of these similarities and differences. We are resources for one another, sharing our wisdom and inspiring one another as we move forward in our lives. We came together tonight to find out what we can expect to gain by participating in a Women Connected coaching group.

1:00 A CLOSER LOOK—WOMEN CONNECTED COACHING GROUP (10 MINUTES)
Now let's take a closer look at the descriptions of the 11 Women Connected coaching sessions and the overall structure of the group.

Distribute Handouts 1.1, 1.2, 1.3.

During the next 10 minutes I'd like you to read the three handouts that I've distributed. The first handout, "Women Connected Outcomes and Benefits," outlines what you can realistically expect to achieve as we move forward with Women Connected. The second handout, "Women Connected 11-Session Coaching Guide," describes the structure that will make it all happen. Eleven sessions, $2\frac{1}{2}$ hours in length, each designed to provide new insights and opportunities for learning about yourself and others in the group. The third handout, "Women Connected Structure," describes the recurring elements that add to the continuity of the program and promote a supportive environment. After we've read the handouts, we'll have a brief discussion.

Group Guide sets the digital timer for 10 minutes. If everyone seems to be finished before 10 minutes has passed, begin the Large Group Discussion early.

1:10 A CLOSER LOOK
LARGE GROUP DISCUSSION (10 MINUTES)

We've had time to read these descriptive Women Connected handouts; what do you think about the processes described? Are there any questions? Keep in mind that I'm new at this, too!

Allow this to be a free flowing discussion. It's important for everyone to feel that what she says will be listened to by the group, and that she has something of value to share. When the discussion seems to be complete (not to exceed 10 minutes), proceed to the next activity.

1:20 MY WISH LIST (20 MINUTES)
Distribute Handout 1.4

Our last activity looks at the areas you might be interested in exploring if you were to commit to going forward with this Women Connected group. Imagine for a moment that anything is possible. With that thought in mind, read this Wish List. After you've read through the statements, place a check mark next to three of the statements you're most interested in at this time of your life. Take a couple of minutes to do this. You will be sharing your responses with a partner in a few minutes.

Group reads handout. Wait until everyone has completed the task. Then say:
Choose one out of your three checked statements that would have the greatest impact if you decided to take action on it beginning tomorrow.

Pick a partner, preferably the person in this group with whom you're least familiar.

Group Guide participates in all activities.

Wait until everyone has a partner and then say:
One of you will be Partner A; the other will be Partner B. Take a moment to decide on your roles. *(Pause)* For this activity, Partner

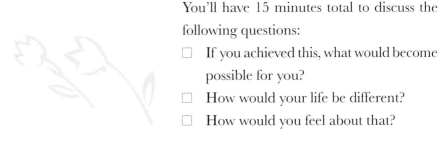

B will go first.

You'll have 15 minutes total to discuss the following questions:

- ☐ If you achieved this, what would become possible for you?
- ☐ How would your life be different?
- ☐ How would you feel about that?

I'll be the timekeeper for this activity and let you know when half the time has expired.

After 7½ minutes, tell the group that it's time to switch speakers and for Partner A to share her information. When a total of 15 minutes is up, take a moment to wrap up this activity. Group Guide gives a one minute warning to complete the conversation.

1:40 MY WISH LIST
LARGE GROUP DISCUSSION (15 MINUTES)
Group Guide facilitates discussion.

What did you notice about yourself and your partner during this activity?

Take a few responses from the group. It's perfectly acceptable for Group Guide to make comments. Just make certain that you do not monopolize the conversation, and encourage all group members to speak.

This is what Women Connected is all about—intentional conversations designed to provoke thinking, open up possibilities, and connect with one another in a supportive, safe environment. Women Connected is facilitated by each of us. We rotate Group Guide responsibilities from session to session so that we each have ownership in the process.

We have one last part of this evening's session, and that is Closing Circle. After the Circle, those of you who want to continue with Women Connected please stay for a few minutes and we'll get our calendars together and set a date for our next session.

1:55 CLOSING CIRCLE (10 MINUTES)

At the end of every Women Connected session, a formal completion takes place. The women in the group stand up and together form a circle. The circle is a universal symbol of unity and wholeness. Since ancient times people have gathered in circles to share stories, provide support, and gain understanding of the common good. This is a special time of closure for the group. Please form a circle, standing shoulder to shoulder. Look around the circle to acknowledge the wisdom within each of us. Let's take a moment to reflect on what mattered most to us during this Evening of Exploration session. Share a word or brief thought that captures your experience of our time together tonight. After each woman has finished, please extinguish your candle. I will go first.

After the last woman has shared, Group Guide says:
Thank you for joining us this evening. It feels wonderful to be together in this way.

2:05 WHAT'S NEXT—NEW BEGINNINGS (25 MINUTES)

Initiate a discussion regarding who will be participating in Women Connected. Make sure to get everyone's contact information. If there are enough women to create a group, decide on the date and time for your first official Women Connected coaching group. If you don't have enough women, you have several options. You can host another Evening of Exploration, meet informally with several new women, or advertise in community bulletins for the purpose of reaching out to more women.

Our evening has almost come to an end. It is time to decide who would like to commit to being in this Women Connected group. Once we know who wants to go forward, we will set up the next time, date, and place to meet. Then during the next session we'll decide how often we'll meet, what timeframe, and what will be our guiding principles.

Some of you might decide that this is not the time for you to join Women Connected, and we fully understand. We want women who can fully commit to being together and growing together over the next 10 sessions.

If you are going forward, here's what to do next. Ask for a volunteer to be the Group Guide for the next session. Remind the group that each group member will take on the role of Group Guide at least once during the next 10 sessions. Instruct the members to take out their calendars and find a date that is available for the next session.

The Group Guide then says:

Our next session will be hosted by *(Group Guide's name)*, on *(date)*, at *(Group Guide's home)*, beginning promptly at *(time)*. New Beginnings is the topic for our next session. In order to prepare for this session and maximize our time together, the Session Accelerator: All About Me needs to be completed in advance. This Session Accelerator will take approximately 30 minutes to complete. You will be sharing this information with the group. Please make a copy of your completed All About Me for each group member. And to help us get to know each other better, please bring a special object that has great significance to you. We'll be sharing this during Check-In at our first session. *(Pass out Session Accelerators 2.1 and 2.2.)*

Afterthoughts

Congratulations! You've now completed your first Women Connected session. How did it go? What did you like most about the session? What learning do you want to take forward into New Beginnings, your first official session as a Women Connected group?

Please don't be concerned if the session had a few bumps along the way. It would be highly unusual for everything to go smoothly the first time. As you discover what works best with your group, you'll incorporate those insights into the following session. Just think how well the group will be functioning by the time you've reached Chapter 11, Celebrating Us!

By now you're ready to go forward with your group, or you're in the process of deciding whom to invite to make your Women Connected group complete. I want to applaud you for starting this life-enhancing journey. You'll find the next session, New Beginnings, is a fabulous foundation for supporting you on your path to personal growth and greater fulfillment in your life.

We don't need someone to show us the ropes.
We are the ones we've been waiting for.
Deep inside us we know the feelings we need to
guide us. Our task is to learn to trust our
inner knowing.

☐ SONIA JOHNSON

Handout 1.1

WOMEN CONNECTED OUTCOMES & BENEFITS

☐ Discover your true purpose and reconnect to your passions

☐ Engage in honest, open, and intentional conversations

☐ Expand and create an exciting vision of what's possible

☐ Identify and alter self-talk that inhibits goal achievement

☐ Liberate yourself from old patterns that hold you back

☐ Create an action plan and achieve profound results

☐ Set up a system of accountability to support your future vision

☐ Put your dreams into motion

☐ Celebrate the accomplishments of others and yourself

☐ Make lifelong friends and have fun

Handout 1.2
WOMEN CONNECTED 11-SESSION COACHING GUIDE

1. **An Evening of Exploration.** Learn about the Women Connected group process and decide whether this is the group for you.
2. **New Beginnings.** Build trust, form group values, and share individual concerns.
3. **Seasons of My Life.** Promote deeper understanding among group members by sharing life stories.
4. **Calling on Purpose.** Identify and clearly define your purpose in life.
5. **Future Perfect.** Create a rich and expansive vision for the coming year.
6. **Dreams in Motion.** Develop goals and support systems to turn dreams into reality.
7. **The Mythology of Me.** Explore belief systems and the stories we tell ourselves that limit possibilities in life.
8. **The Brand of Me.** Define how you want to show up in the world—how you want to be perceived.
9. **Breaking Through Obstacles.** Discover ways to break through limiting beliefs.
10. **Courageous Conversations.** Practice delivering the difficult message and, with the group's support, communicate that message to the person to whom you need to speak.
11. **Celebrating Us!** Celebrate the accomplishments, changes, and breakthroughs resulting from your time in Women Connected.

Handout 1.3
WOMEN CONNECTED STRUCTURE

POEM
A poem is selected ahead of time by the Group Guide. It is read at the beginning of each session to set the tone and provide a time to settle in, quiet the mind, and connect the group. You will find a large selection of poetry books in the Resources section at the back of this book.

CHECK-IN
This time is scheduled at the beginning of each session to connect with the group. Group members share updates on their commitments, challenges, and accomplishments. Questions for Check-In might include:
- What results are showing up in my life that I like?
- What results are showing up that I don't like?
- What have been my lessons this month?

After each woman completes her Check-In, she lights a candle and states her intention for the session.

FOCUS OF THE SESSION
Each session will focus on a specific topic that accelerates personal growth and supports movement toward a clearly defined vision.

WISDOM BLAST
This is a process designed to access the group's collective wisdom. Each woman has the option to bring an issue, challenge, or dilemma before the group. For three minutes the group generates as many ideas as possible to help address the issue. This is the only time when giving advice is encouraged. The advice is captured by a scribe, and the recipient of the group's wisdom reports the results of the Wisdom Blast by e-mail or phone, or at the next Check-In.

CAPTURING WHAT MATTERS MOST TO ME

The learnings, insights, and memories from each session are documented in a personal journal or the specially designed handout at the end of each chapter. This process helps to re-focus on what was covered during the session and tracks the personal growth of each individual.

MY COMMITMENTS

During each session time is set aside to write commitments aligned with each woman's purpose and clearly defined vision for the year. Clarifying each woman's purpose and vision will take place in sessions included in the Women Connected program.

GROWTH BUDDIES

At the end of each session, each woman is assigned one person who will be her Growth Buddy until the next session. Growth Buddies support each other in honoring their commitments, act as sounding boards when necessary, and cheer each other on between sessions.

CLOSING CIRCLE

At the end of every Women Connected session, there is a formal completion ceremony. The women in the group stand up and together form a circle, the universal symbol of unity and wholeness. Since ancient times people have gathered in circles to share stories, provide support, and gain understanding of the common good. This is a special time of closure for the group. In the Closing Circle, each woman shares a word or brief thought that expresses what she learned or how she was affected by the session. After she shares her experience, she extinguishes her candle and the session is complete.

PLANNING THE NEXT SESSION

After the Closing Circle the arrangements for the next session are discussed. A decision is made on the next session date, who the Group Guide will be, and the location. Growth Buddies are assigned to work with one another between sessions during this time. The Session Accelerator (the preparation work for the next session) is distributed.

Handout 1.4
MY WISH LIST

Please place a check mark next to three of the following statements to which you're most drawn. Then choose one out of your three checked statements that would have the greatest impact in your life *if you took direct action to address it.*

- ☐ Enhance personal effectiveness
- ☐ Create more fulfillment in my life
- ☐ Nurture and express my inner voice
- ☐ Clarify my purpose and vision
- ☐ Make my dreams come true
- ☐ Release old patterns and behaviors that keep me stuck
- ☐ Expand my problem-solving skills
- ☐ Enhance my communication skills
- ☐ Deepen my relationships
- ☐ Increase my creativity
- ☐ Enhance my effectiveness in dealing with others
- ☐ Reduce conflict in work and personal relationships
- ☐ Engage in more self-care activities
- ☐ Have fun and celebrate achievements

Session Accelerator 2.1
A SPECIAL OBJECT

Bring a special object that has great significance to you. We'll be sharing this during Check-In at our first session together, New Beginnings.

Session Accelerator 2.2
ALL ABOUT ME

Complete the following statements. This information will be shared with the group as a way of introducing what works for you and what doesn't.

☐ The best ways to offer support to me are:

☐ The ways I like to be affirmed and validated are:

☐ I prefer to receive feedback in the following ways:

Please make a copy of your All About Me information for each woman in your group. You'll keep this information with other important material in your notebook. If everyone has a copy for each member in the group, it can be referred to when working with your Growth Buddy. You'll find this to be very valuable information in working with one another over the course of the remaining sessions.

New
Beginnings

One day you finally knew what you had to do, and began.

□ MARY OLIVER

A new beginning is always exciting. It's a fresh start, a time to leave old judgments and assessments behind, to start a new chapter in life. Now that you and your friends have made a firm decision to join together in a journey of growth and self-exploration, this session offers a time to enjoy the anticipation that always accompanies the unknown. Although some of you may already know each other outside this group, you have never come together in quite this way before. As with any new beginning, anything's possible!

When beginning a new group, it's helpful to know a little bit about the stages that groups naturally go through over time in their formation and development. Each stage has a name and recognizable behaviors that show up during the process. Forming, Storming, and Norming are three stages that groups commonly go though in their development.

The first stage, which you have just entered, is called Forming. Sometimes it's called the honeymoon period, when all the group members are happy with each other. The first issues a group deals with are related to acceptance *(Do I belong here?)*, building trust *(Can I trust these women?)*, and creating a safe environment *(Can I express myself fully here without being judged?)*.

The second stage of group development is called Storming. This stage, when the honeymoon ends, will most likely take place by the fourth or fifth session. It is for this reason that halfway though the Women Connected program, between Chapter 5, Future Perfect, and Chapter 6, Dreams in Motion, there is an assessment activity designed to assist the group in doing a mid-course tune-up. Every successful relationship or group has one thing in common: open and honest dialogue. Healthy dialogue means addressing what's working and what's not working, considering realistic suggestions, and taking action together toward positive change. During this stage, questions arise: *If I disagree with you, will I be judged or will you accept my differences? Do I feel heard and valued or do I feel out of sync with the group? Is this group able to accommodate the diversity of the women within it? How do we deal with conflict? Does tension go underground or do we bring issues forward and deal with them respectfully?* All these questions need to be addressed as you progress on this journey of growth together.

The final stage of group development is called Norming. At this stage the initial bonding of belonging has deepened, and the women in the group are more comfortable with who they are and how they connect with each other. The group has agreed on what works, smoothed the bumps in the road, and is now moving forward at a comfortable pace. The members are focused on supporting each other's strengths, rather than focusing on differences. In the Norming stage, things are very good. By overcoming difficulties together, the group has learned that all members can be themselves without hesitation or worry, and share their journey over time. This is the stage when action is accelerated and *real* collaboration becomes the norm of the group.

Group development typically does not proceed along a linear path. It is cyclic in nature and you can count on it changing over time. With determination and commitment to each other, you'll be just fine with whatever comes up. The New Beginnings session is an opportunity to look at your life and your world with fresh eyes and to access wisdom that wasn't available to you before. Your group is giving birth to something unique, and in this first session you'll begin to discover what it means to focus on a powerful intention together.

Words of Wisdom

GETTING READY FOR YOUR FIRST WOMEN CONNECTED SESSION

When you arrive give yourself a few moments, even if it's just sitting in your car or standing and looking at the sky. Take a few deep breaths, be present, and leave the outside world behind even before you enter. How you enter (rushing and breathless, or calm and centered) says a lot about what you intend to bring to your Women Connected group.

BE GENTLE WITH YOURSELF AND OTHERS

Even something good can involve stress. You might feel more quiet and reserved than usual. Conversely, you might find you're more talkative than usual, filling the space with words to ease your discomfort. First times are awkward; do you remember your first date? You might have had the feeling of butterflies in your stomach, sweaty palms, or a racing heart. I know I did. Focusing on the rhythm of your breathing works well to quiet your mind and bring yourself present to the conversation, and it also helps you to be gentle with yourself and others.

Bumps in the Road—With Solutions!

LOSING TRACK OF TIME

It's especially important in this first session that the Group Guide keeps track of the time allotted for activities, and that the group starts and ends on time.

Solution: Rather than assigning just one person to be a Time Cop, it's usually best to have the group as a whole assume accountability for the suggested timeframes, rotating Timekeeper responsibilities for each activity. The way time is handled in this first session is crucial. Trust me: If this particular area remains loose and sloppy, the group will end up feeling there's never enough time to do what you set out to do. More than once in a Women Connected group, I've watched our time spin out of control, and it's no picnic. To avoid frustration, each group member begins the session with a strong commitment to honoring the time allotted for each activity, and to supporting the Timekeeper. To accomplish the goals of the group, remain focused on the task at hand.

WHEN SOMEONE FORGETS THE SESSION ACCELERATOR

From time to time someone will forget to bring her Session Accelerator or forget to take time to complete it before the session.

Solution: If this happens in your group, you have at least three options.

- ☐ The woman with the incomplete Session Accelerator can arrive early and complete the assignment.

- ☐ She can spontaneously respond to the questions as if she had completed them.

- ☐ The entire group can take time out for silence, meditation, or personal journal writing while the woman completes her assignment.

This third option would increase the length of the session, so the group would need to agree to it. Whichever option you choose, it is always a good idea to remember that the Session Accelerator is crucial to the session's success. However, it's also important not to make anyone wrong for not completing her assignment—stuff happens!

Darlene's Story

A decisive, strong, take-charge kind of gal and a natural-born leader, Darlene spent the first 25 years of her career as a Registered Nurse in the Labor and Delivery room of a large urban hospital. Happily married for 31 years, she had met her husband at work. As she puts it, he was her "first adult relationship."

Life was going well and all seemed perfect, until her daughter reached 13 years. Suddenly it was as though a new person had shown up in the house, and Darlene's "pride and joy" began making decisions that shook the family's foundation to its core. Her daughter's experimentation with drugs and alcohol, her wild behavior and life-threatening choices called for an extreme solution. Within six months of the first incident of her daughter's disregard for parental authority, Darlene and her husband made arrangements for a family intervention, and their daughter was admitted to an intensive residential program for teens. Every parent with a child in this program was required to participate in personal growth seminars and parenting classes. Over the next two years, there were times of joy and hope, and lengthy periods that Darlene described as "just plain hell."

A lot of good came out of this tumultuous period. The family repaired old hurts, worked through disappointments, and forgave one another for their mistakes. Darlene learned that she needed an outlet for herself, a place where she could create new friendships, explore dreams, and open her heart to receive acceptance and support. She knew that to move on in her life, she needed to look beyond her roles as a wife, mother, and nurse. Darlene had never allowed herself to have friendships with women. All of her time had been devoted to work and to caring for her husband and her daughter. She had spent 40 years hiding out from herself, and had a deep fear of what she might discover.

Darlene had heard about Women Connected through a friend. Women Connected was a safe place to begin looking, a place to start the journey of self-awareness. During the first session, New Beginnings, Darlene was terribly nervous. She spent most of the time sizing up the other women in the room. Darlene asked herself, *Who can I relate to here? Who will push and challenge me? Who would let me slide, and who will hold me accountable?* But the one thing she remembers most of all is that Women Connected felt safe—right from the beginning.

The Big Picture: New Beginnings

Suggested Time Frames	Activity	Purpose	Materials | Set-up
:05	Opening	Welcome; transition into Women Connected; become present	• Poem
:20	Check-In	Update, reconnect, report	• Candle for each woman • Completed Session Accelerator 2.1 A Special Object
1:45	Session: New Beginnings	Build a sense of identity within the group. Create guidelines for being together and share individual preferences for support and feedback.	• Completed Session Accelerator 2.2 All About Me • Handout 2.1 Women Connected 11-Session Coaching Guide • Handout 2.2 Building Trust Together
:05	Capturing What Matters Most to Me	Highlight session insights that are most relevant to your life	• Personal journal or Handout 2.3 Capturing What Matters Most to Me
:05	My Commitments	Increase accountability, intention, and likelihood of successful goal attainment	• Handout 2.4 My Commitments
:05	Closing Circle	Complete the session	• Standing circle • Extinguish candles • Camera for group photo
:05	Logistics for next session	Ensure Group continuity and clarity of requirements for the next session	• Handout 2.5 Contact Information • Designate Group Guide, time, place • Choose a new Growth Buddy • Session Accelerator 3.1 Seasons of My Life

What Happens During the "New Beginnings" Session

0:00 WELCOME (5 MINUTES)

Prior to starting the group, place a candle for each woman near the location where the group will be gathered. Each woman will light a candle at the completion of her Check-In.

Group Guide says:

Welcome to our first official Women Connected coaching session. I anticipate that by the end of our time together we'll have created a solid foundation for moving forward with our dreams and personal ambitions. We'll start with a couple of minutes of silence. The purpose is to quiet our minds, become present to what's possible today, and shift our focus to intentional conversations. Let's begin by taking three to four deep breaths. As you inhale, breathe deeply into all the possibilities that are waiting for you to discover. As you exhale, sink deeply into your authentic self and relax into a state of openness and connection to self, and become present to new possibilities.

Group Guide reads her preselected poem.

After the poem is read say:

Silently affirm to yourself the intention you're holding for this session. How will you show up in today's session, what will you contribute, and how will you demonstrate your support in the group?

What You'll Need

- Poem
- Candle for each woman
- Digital timer
- Personal journal or notebook
- Calendar for setting next session's date
- Camera for group photo
- Completed Session Accelerator 2.1 A Special Object
- Completed Session Accelerator 2.2 All About Me
- Handout 2.1 Women Connected 11-Session Coaching Guide
- Handout 2.2 Building Trust Together
- Handout 2.3 Capturing What Matters Most to Me
- Handout 2.4 My Commitments
- Handout 2.5 Contact Information
- Session Accelerator 3.1 Seasons of My Life

Session Accelerator and handouts are provided as downloadable files at www.WomenConnected.com

Allow one minute of quiet reflection and then proceed to Check-In.

0:05 CHECK-IN (20 MINUTES)

Let's begin our first Women Connected Check-In. Since this is our first official time together, our Check-In will be structured in a unique way.

Each of us will respond to the following question:

☐ If a close friend were to introduce you, what would that person be likely to say about you?

After you have responded to this question, you will then share the special object that you brought and describe its meaning and significance. After each of us completes her Check-In, she'll light a candle and place her special object in the center of the group (or in a designated place). This is a meaningful ritual that signifies we are bringing ourselves to this group and coming together in a special environment that will produce new possibilities. We'll engage in intentional conversations and support one another in creating the lives we desire. We'll each have about two minutes for our Check-In. I'll go first.

Remember that the Group Guide will model the time frame on Check-In. Tell the group that you'll be using the digital timer, and that when the two minutes are up, the next person to her right checks in. Make sure to stay within the two-minute time frame.

As each woman completes her Check-In, she lights a candle and states her intention for the session.

After the Check-In is complete, proceed to the next activity.

0:25 INTRODUCTION TO NEW BEGINNINGS (5 MINUTES)

Today's session is New Beginnings. This session is designed to provide opportunities for us to get to know one another and reflect on why we chose the Women Connected coaching group as the vehicle for our growth and personal development. We'll explore what we'd like to accomplish during the next 10 sessions, and gain an understanding of the structural components of Women Connected. We'll have conversations in small groups and pairs, and we will have time to reflect individually on the issues that are most important to us.

In our session today we will begin to build a sense of identity within the group. We will revisit the Women Connected Coaching Guide session topics, and create our principles for connecting and interacting with each other. We'll define and discuss how we will create a strong foundation of trust that will allow us to build Women Connected together.

0:30 WOMEN CONNECTED 11-SESSION COACHING GUIDE (5 MINUTES)

Distribute Handout 2.1

As you remember from the Evening of Exploration, this handout describes each of the 11 Women Connected Coaching Guide sessions. Please take a moment to reacquaint yourselves with this handout. We have a lot to look forward to!

Tell the group that they'll have a few minutes to read the Women Connected 11-Session Coaching Guide descriptions. In a couple of minutes check to see if everyone has reviewed the 11-session description, and then move on to the next activity.

0:35 CONNECTING PRINCIPLES (20 MINUTES)

In order for Women Connected to be successful, it's important to decide what behaviors are acceptable and how we want to conduct ourselves during our sessions. We'll call them our Connecting Principles. These will be the guidelines that will support a creative, safe, and trusting environment. We need to decide what Connecting Principles must be in place in order for each of us to feel safe, heard, and understood. This will support our learning together.

Some examples of Connecting Principles:
- ☐ Being on time
- ☐ Confidentiality *(Lead a brief discussion and explore how each group member defines confidentiality.)*
- ☐ One person speaks at a time *(Take time and discuss why this would be important.)*

☐ Complete Session Accelerator prior to each session. *(What difference might this make in the results experienced by the group?)*

Group Guide will lead or co-lead a discussion, while a volunteer captures the Connecting Principles in writing. It is imperative that everyone agrees on each and every Principle. Don't assume agreement—take a vote on each Principle. Generally speaking, five to six Connecting Principles are enough to guide the group. It's better to have a smaller number that everyone is absolutely committed to and that can easily be remembered.

We will review these Connecting Principles on a regular basis and add to them and modify them if necessary.

Once agreement is reached on the Connecting Principles, move on to the next activity.

0:55 ALL ABOUT ME (25 MINUTES)

Instruct group to take out completed Session Accelerator 2.2

It's important for each of us to gain understanding on the best ways to offer support and provide feedback for individuals in our group. Each of us listens to information in different ways, and without knowing the specific listening preferences, we would be guessing as to what each woman needs.

Let's take a few minutes to share with the group our responses to the following questions:
☐ The best ways to offer support to me are
☐ The ways I like to be affirmed and validated are
☐ I prefer to receive feedback in the following ways

Who would like to go first? After you have shared your responses to All About Me, distribute copies of your information to each of the group members.

To determine the time available for each woman, divide the number of women present into 25 minutes. Let the group know the time available, and inform them that you'll be setting the digital timer to help move things along.

After the last of the women has shared her responses, Group Guide says:
I'd like to thank you for sharing how you wish to be supported, ways in which you like to be affirmed and validated, and your preference for receiving feedback. As we go through future sessions together, this information will be of great value.

1:20 BUILDING TRUST TOGETHER (10 MINUTES)
Distribute Handout 2.2

Our next activity will address the issue of trust: how it is built, how it is destroyed, and what can be done to reestablish trust when it is broken. We will be doing this activity with a partner. Partner up with the person in the group with whom you are least familiar.

Give the group time to select their partners.

Now that you're with your partner, here are two statements for reflection.
- ☐ I trust people who . . . *(list all the things that people do to create trust with you)*
- ☐ I don't trust people who . . . *(list all the things that people do to break trust with you)*

Take a few minutes to write your individual responses to the statements on your handout. Then, when you and your partner have completed your individual reflections, you'll share your responses with each other.

You'll have 10 minutes to complete the partners' portion of this activity. I'll be the timekeeper and let you know when half the time has passed.

Group Guide, as always, participates in this activity. Set the digital timer for five minutes. When five minutes have passed, instruct group that they have five minutes left for this activity. Reset digital timer for five minutes.

After the second five-minute segment is concluded, facilitate the following discussion.

1:35 BUILDING TRUST TOGETHER
LARGE GROUP DISCUSSION (10 MINUTES)

Who would like to volunteer to record the group's responses? (*Wait until someone volunteers for the task and is ready with paper and pen.*) As we share our responses, when you hear a response similar to yours, please cross it off your list.

After each woman has contributed to the list, engage in a brief discussion, taking no more than five minutes. The following questions might be useful in starting the conversation.

☐ What do you notice about this list?

☐ What part does trust play in our Women Connected group?

After the discussion is complete, thank the group and proceed to the next part of the activity.

1:45 BUILDING TRUST TOGETHER—PART 2
(10 MINUTES)

Now it's time for the second part of this activity. Please find a new partner. *Give them time to select their partners.*

Now that you've selected a new partner, you have two more questions to respond to. Take a minute to write your individual responses to the second set of questions on your handout, and when you and your partner are complete, you'll share your responses with each other. The two questions are:

☐ What are the ways that we can establish trust in this group?

☐ If trust is broken within the group, what will you do to reestablish it?

You'll have 10 minutes to complete this portion of the activity. I'll be the timekeeper and let you know when half the time has passed.

Set the digital timer for five minutes. When five minutes have passed, instruct group that they have five minutes left for this activity. Reset digital timer for five minutes.

After a total of 10 minutes, proceed to the group discussion.

1:55 BUILDING TRUST TOGETHER—PART 2
LARGE GROUP DISCUSSION (10 MINUTES)

Who would like to volunteer to capture the

group's responses? If you hear someone share a response similar to yours, please cross it off your list.

After each woman has contributed to the list, engage in a brief discussion, taking no more than five minutes The following questions might be useful in starting the conversation.

☐ What are the similarities and differences that you heard?

☐ As we begin our work together, what are some of the possibilities you envision?

At the end of the discussion, thank the group for their insights and contributions to the topic of trust building in the group. Then proceed to the next activity.

2:05 CAPTURING WHAT MATTERS MOST TO ME (5 MINUTES)
Distribute Handout 2.3

At the end of each Women Connected coaching session, we will spend up to five minutes capturing our memories. The purpose for doing this activity is to ensure that we keep track of the changes in our lives, the challenges we face together, and the lessons learned from session to session. Please take out your personal journal or use the handout. Let's capture our thoughts about this session while they are fresh in our minds.

As you journal about this session, you might ask yourself:

☐ What was most valuable to me in this session?

☐ Regarding this session, what are my thoughts, feelings, or reactions?

☐ I contributed to the group when I:

I'll be the timekeeper and set the digital timer for five minutes.

When time is up, you might ask:

Would anyone like to share one of your comments with the group?

Take a minute or two to listen to a few comments, and then continue on to the next activity.

2:10 MY COMMITMENTS (5 MINUTES)
Distribute Handout 2.4

Commitments provide energy, drive, direction, and purpose in life. They help you procrastinate less and become more action-oriented. Commitments are critical to producing successful and healthy change in your life. Today you will be choosing one commitment. This will be something that you can complete prior to our next session. Challenge yourself and have it be something that really matters. It might be something you have been putting off or thought was too difficult. Making weekly commitments will be an on-going practice in this group. After a few sessions, when we have completed work on our purpose and vision for the year, the commitments that you make will be aligned with the life you choose to create this year and into the future. In silence, please take a few minutes to reflect on and write down your commitments.

After everyone has written her commitment, say:

We'll take a few minutes and share our commitments with each other. Start by stating your commitment and why it is important to you at this time in your life. Who would like to go first?

After the last woman has shared her commitment, thank the group and proceed to the next activity.

2:15 GROWTH BUDDIES (5 MINUTES)

As a way to support each other between sessions, we will be selecting what the Women Connected coaching program calls a Growth Buddy. The responsibility of the Growth Buddy is to support you between sessions, hold you accountable for your commitments, and be a sounding board when you need someone to talk to. At the end of each session, you will select a new Growth Buddy. This will give everyone the opportunity to be paired with each person in the group.

For additional information on Growth Buddies, refer to pages 240-246 in the Resources section at the back of this book.

Select a partner to be your Growth Buddy.

When there are an odd number of group members, it is okay for three women to be Growth Buddies.

Take a few minutes with your Growth Buddy and decide the best times to connect between now and our next session. Make a commitment to have two or more contacts with each other. The connection can take place in person, through e-mail, or by telephone calls. You will be asked at the next session to report on how things went with your Growth Buddy.

After five minutes thank the group and proceed to the Closing Circle.

2:20 CLOSING CIRCLE (5 MINUTES)

This is a special time of closure for the group. The circle represents a universal symbol of unity and wholeness.

As we come to the end of this session, let's stand and form a circle. Take a moment to think of a word or brief thought that expresses what you experienced in the New Beginnings session.

Rotating around the circle, each woman shares her word or thought. After everyone has shared in Closing Circle, say:
This session is complete. Please extinguish your candle until we connect again.

Take a group photo at the end of Closing Circle.

2:25 WHAT'S NEXT—SEASONS OF MY LIFE (5 MINUTES)

Ask for a volunteer to be the Group Guide for the next session. Remind the group that each group member will take on the role of Group Guide at least once during the next nine sessions. Invite everyone to take out her calendar to find an available date for the next session.

Our next session will be hosted by *(Group Guide)*, on *(date)*, at *(Group Guide's home)*, beginning promptly at *(time)*.

Seasons of My Life is the topic for our next session. In order to prepare for this session and maximize our time together, the Seasons Timeline needs to be completed in advance.

This Session Accelerator will take approximately one hour to complete. Each of us will be given approximately 10-12 minutes to share her Seasons of My Life Timeline with the group. *(Pass out Session Accelerator 3.1.)*

Please make sure to complete your Contact Information, Handout 2.5, before you leave today. I will make copies for everyone prior to our next session.

Afterthoughts

You are building the foundation for a powerful Women Connected experience. You've made decisions about how you want to engage with one another, and made commitments to adhere to your Connecting Principles. You've learned how the women in your group want to be supported, including the best way to give feedback to each individual. The critical component of group success—trust—has been addressed, so that any future conflicts can be handled with the variety of solutions that were brought forth today. You've now experienced all the key elements of a Women Connected session and are ready to proceed to the next session, Seasons of My Life. During this session you'll hear one another's stories and listen to each woman's challenges and accomplishments. You'll be amazed at the supportive environment your group is creating in such a short period of time. Canadian author Lucy Maud Montgomery reminds us what is possible as we go forward together when she writes, "There is so much in the world for us all if we only have the eyes to see it, and the heart to love it, and the hand to gather it to ourselves."

Handout 2.1
WOMEN CONNECTED 11-SESSION COACHING GUIDE OUTLINE

1. **An Evening of Exploration.** Learn about the Women Connected group process and decide whether this is the group for you.
2. **New Beginnings.** Build trust, form group values, and share individual concerns.
3. **Seasons of My Life.** Promote deeper understanding among group members by sharing life stories.
4. **Calling on Purpose.** Identify and clearly define your purpose in life.
5. **Future Perfect.** Create a rich and expansive vision for the coming year.
6. **Dreams in Motion.** Develop goals and support systems to turn dreams into reality.
7. **The Mythology of Me**. Explore belief systems and the stories we tell ourselves that limit possibilities in life.
8. **The Brand of Me.** Define how you want to show up in the world—how you want to be perceived.
9. **Breaking Through Obstacles.** Discover ways to break through limiting beliefs.
10. **Courageous Conversations.** Practice delivering the difficult message and, with the group's support, communicate that message to the person to whom you need to speak.
11. **Celebrating Us!** Celebrate the accomplishments, changes, and breakthroughs resulting from your time in Women Connected.

Handout 2.2

BUILDING TRUST TOGETHER

Write your individual responses to the following statements.

☐ I trust people who . . . *(list all the things that people do to create trust with you)*

☐ I don't trust people who . . . *(list all the things that people do to break trust with you)*

After you have shared your responses with a partner, write your answers to the following questions.

☐ What are the ways that we can establish trust in this group?

☐ If trust is broken within the group what will you do to reestablish it?

Handout 2.3

CAPTURING WHAT MATTERS MOST TO ME

☐ What was most valuable to you in this session?

☐ Regarding this session, what are your thoughts, feelings, or reactions?

☐ I contributed to the group when I

Handout 2.4
MY COMMITMENTS

Trust that still, small voice that says,
"This might work and I'll try it."

☐ DIANE MARIECHILD

Today's Date _____

Commitment _____
_____
_____

Date completed _____

Commitment _____
_____
_____

Date completed _____

Commitment _____
_____
_____

Date completed _____

Handout 2.5

CONTACT INFORMATION

Name _____

Address _____

_____

_____

_____

Home Phone _____

Work Phone _____

Mobile _____

Fax _____

E-mail address _____

Birthday _____

Session Accelerator 3.1

SEASONS OF MY LIFE

PURPOSE: To connect and build trust within the group by sharing life experiences. This activity acts as a concentrated autobiography for each woman. It is a valuable tool in understanding the past experiences, accomplishments, difficult times, and significant events of the members of your group.

PROCESS: Reflect on your life over the last several decades. Remember the highlights, challenges, celebrations, accomplishments, losses, and adventures; the peaks and the valleys of your life. (You'll find some suggestions for reflection at the bottom of this Session Accelerator.) What learning did you take from each decade? Who were the people that influenced and guided you during each period? Begin at 10 years of age.

On a large sheet of paper (11 by 14 inches) draw a graph that represents The Seasons of My Life. With the horizontal middle of the paper as the neutral zone, mark each of the significant memories in a way that reflects its variance from neutral.

☐ Does your graph look like a series of mountains and valleys?

☐ Does your life graph look fairly even across the decades?

☐ Do some of the decades look different than others?

☐ As you review your life, what are the patterns and themes?

☐ What do you think your life has been about?

☐ What, if anything, is missing?

SUGGESTIONS FOR REFLECTION

Think about family changes, marriage, children, divorce, death, mentors, teachers, education, career/job changes, religious/spiritual experiences, travel/vacation, hobbies/sports, holidays, recreation, moves, role of music/literature/art, or anything else that will trigger your memories.

Seasons of My
Life

Just to be alive is a grand thing.

□ AGATHA CHRISTIE

We connect by sharing the stories of our lives. By listening deeply to one another, we discover our similarities and learn to appreciate our differences. Trust is built when openness in communication and vulnerability are shared within the group. It can be scary in the beginning; it becomes easier with each session. When we share the histories of our lives, an incredible bond is formed and authenticity emerges.

Women often forget how much we have accomplished and how much we have learned from our past relationships. Typically we focus on the future, and spend little time acknowledging our achievements. Too often we forget our greatness. Some of us spend time comparing ourselves to others, and feel that we'll never measure up. Some of us identify ourselves by what material goods we possess, forgetting who we really are and what really matters. We may spend time supporting friends and family while

67

letting our own needs and desires fall into neglect. Taking time to reflect on the past and to notice—really notice—all that we are and all that we've done brings a renewed sense of understanding and compassion for how we have lived our lives up to this moment. While it's not necessary to dwell on the past, it can be important simply to take a look at your life so far, to see the connections, to understand what's transpired, and then move on to whatever is coming up next.

When my youngest child graduated from high school, I decided it was time for me to graduate as well! A high school teacher and school counselor for many years, I now felt it was time to move on to something new. I wasn't sure what this something new would look like, but I did know that whatever it was, I'd be learning and growing from it. I must admit I liked the idea of eating in a restaurant now and then, rather than frequenting the high school cafeteria on a regular basis.

A couple of years before leaving the school district, I had started a part time consulting practice with another school counselor. Diann and I thought it would be fun to work with small businesses in our community. So during summers and school vacations we taught communication courses, facilitated team-building activities, and presented programs at conferences throughout the country. I enjoyed our partnership and began to imagine what it would be like to work full time as a consultant. In all these daydreams, Diann and I were working side by side. But life loves to surprise us, and when I left the school district Diann decided to stay. We both knew her decision was absolutely the right one for her.

Because I was determined to leave high school counseling before burnout set in, I left before I was fully prepared to go. In retrospect it may not have been the best way to proceed, but it was my way at the time. Starting a new career was a challenging task. I had a few contacts, but not enough consulting work to pay the bills. Very soon I began to question my decision and, one after another, negative thoughts crept in. What was I thinking? I had no experience in the business world! What did I think I could offer to potential clients? One particularly convincing acquaintance continued to insist, "Educators just don't understand the world of business!" Something was needed to shake up my thinking. It was then that I remembered how valuable it had been at other times in my life to create a Seasons of My Life timeline.

I decided to focus on my education and work history, charting my life experience according to my various roles and responsibilities over time. And the most interesting thing happened! As I began to look at the patterns—my life choices and the various jobs I had held—I got reacquainted with my strengths, my gifts, and my successes. I felt not only relief, but a sense of real strength and pride. Sure, there had been occasional slumps, but as I looked over the "Seasons" timeline, it was clear that I hadn't been giving myself enough credit. Around this time I heard about a consulting firm that was seeking trainers. I applied, was hired, and soon realized that, as an educator, I had plenty of experience in the real world and a great deal of value to contribute. From time to time in our women's group, we chart our life path to re-remember all that we have done. Then we begin to look ahead, speaking about the future that we will be creating.

Speaking our truths, sharing our stories, and tapping into our innate wisdom, creates a solid foundation for group success. In my history as a facilitator of Women Connected groups, these are the experiences that most effectively motivate us to be our best selves. Connecting deeply and honestly with group members, supports the acceleration of personal and professional growth.

This is your time. Deeply reconnect with yourself and others in purposeful ways.

Today we will share our life experiences from 10 years of age. This activity represents a concentrated autobiography for each woman. It is a trust-building activity and will acquaint you with the peaks and valleys of your own and others' lives. You'll discover how the past has affected who and what you are today. You'll revisit some of the lessons learned, and re-remember decisions made and results produced.

As a result of this process, you and the women in your group will deepen your knowledge of one another; connect with each others' passions, challenges, and heartbreaks; begin to see different life choices and the results of those choices; and come to an understanding of what "women connected" means to your group. I've done this activity countless times, and every time I find myself profoundly affected by the courage, compassion, and resiliency that we women possess. When the depth of group wisdom is brought to the surface, it sparkles like a million twinkling stars. When women connect with purpose in intentional conversations, the possibilities are infinite.

Words of Wisdom

WATCH THE TIME

It's easy to get so wrapped up in someone's story that 30 minutes go by and she's got a couple of decades left to share!

This has happened in my groups many times. Make certain that you don't short-change the activity, but at the same time it shouldn't last for eight hours! Remember the importance of honoring everyone's time. It is good to practice being succinct in your communication—getting to the heart of the matter without communicating *every* detail.

Before you begin, let the group decide together how much time each person will be given to tell their story. Then ask for a volunteer to be the timekeeper, so that only one of you will need to watch the clock. After each woman completes her story, pass the timekeeper role to a new woman.

Bumps in the Road—With Solutions!

DIFFICULTY LISTENING AND LOSING FOCUS

After listening to the life stories of four to five women, you notice that you're losing concentration and focus.

Solution: If you are feeling this way, it's likely that others in the group are feeling the same. Suggest a short stretch break, and return to the group refreshed. It's great practice to ask for what is needed.

SOMEONE INTERRUPTING THE SPEAKER OR ASKING A CLARIFYING QUESTION

It is not uncommon to want to ask questions when someone is sharing her life experiences. In fact, it can be a challenge to sit, listen, and not say a word.

Solution: If you find yourself wanting to interrupt or ask a question about someone's experiences, take a deep breath, refocus, and put the question aside. After the session is complete, if you still want to ask the question, feel free to do so.

Freddie Lyn's Story

An athletic woman with short auburn hair and freckles, Freddie Lyn always struck me as being quite a bit taller than her five feet three inches. A hiker and biker, an avid skier, and a tireless student of life, she is 57 years young. Freddie Lyn is one of those people who's always ready to pitch in and help with a smile. In her church she does volunteer work with middle-school youth.

As you might guess, Freddie Lyn has always been a fairly independent, self-reliant woman. She never formed many close relationships with other women because she didn't feel the need for them. After a 30-year career in high tech sales and management, however, she felt she had been living in a man's world and she

longed for collaborative connections with other women, in whose company she could learn and grow.

In Women Connected, Freddie Lyn confessed that she had felt hurt and judged by women in the past, and for this reason had resisted trusting them. During this session of Women Connected, the process of looking at her life in 10-year increments showed Freddie Lyn that, although she had succeeded wildly in her career, her life was almost devoid of close relationships. Even her family felt remote to her. She said that in many ways she was like a toddler; she wasn't sure how to begin. It was during the Seasons of My Life session that Freddie Lyn made a commitment to create more close relationships in her life.

She joined a women's business organization, and gradually began to intentionally develop and nurture friendships with the women she met there. Two years later, Freddie Lyn launched her own leadership development and coaching company. Her business, founded on principles of partnering and collaborating with other coaches and consultants, has been a phenomenal success.

While recently participating in a cultural business exchange program, Freddie Lyn had the opportunity to connect with young businesswomen in the Baltic States.

The connections she made resulted in her mentoring two businesswomen from Romania. Today, Freddie Lyn continues to form significant relationships with like-minded women who are interested in professional and personal development. Her life is thriving, and from her perspective, "life is good". And so it is.

The Big Picture: Seasons of My Life

Suggested Time Frames	Activity	Purpose	Materials | Set-up
:05	Opening	Welcome; transition into Women Connected; become present	• Poem
:20	Check-In	Update, reconnect, report	• Candle for each woman
1:45	Session: Seasons of My Life	Deepen knowledge and appreciation of who members are and what unique gifts they bring to the group	• Completed Session Accelerator 3.1 Seasons of My Life
:05	Capturing What Matters Most to Me	Highlight session insights that are most relevant to your life	• Personal journal or Handout 3.1 Capturing What Matters Most to Me
:05	My Commitments	Increase accountability, intention, and likelihood of successful goal attainment	• Handout 3.2 My Commitments
:05	Closing Circle	Complete the session	• Standing circle • Extinguish candles
:05	Logistics for next session	Ensure Group continuity and clarity of requirements for the next session	• Designate Group Guide, time, place • Choose a new Growth Buddy • Session Accelerator 4.1 Excavating Purpose

What You'll Need

- Poem
- Candle for each woman
- Digital timer
- Personal journal or notebook
- Calendar for setting next session's date
- Session Accelerator 3.1 Seasons of My Life
- Handout 3.1 Capturing What Matters Most to Me
- Handout 3.2 My Commitments
- Session Accelerator 4.1 Excavating Purpose

Session Accelerator and handouts are provided as downloadable files at www.WomenConnected.com

What Happens During the "Seasons of My Life" Session

0:00 WELCOME (5 MINUTES)

Prior to starting the group, place a candle for each woman near the location where the group will be gathered. Each woman will light a candle at the completion of her Check-In.

Group Guide welcomes everyone to her home and this session.

Inform the group that there will be a couple of minutes of silence. The purpose is to quiet the mind, get present, and shift focus to intentional conversations. Let's begin by taking three or four deep breaths. Drop your shoulders, feel your feet firmly on the ground, and just settle into this moment in time. Now as you take your next breath, inhale all that is possible, and slowly exhale any tension or tightness in your body.

Group Guide reads her preselected poem.

After the poem is read say:
Silently affirm to yourself the intention you're holding for this session. How will you show up in today's session, what will you contribute, and how will you demonstrate your support to the group?

Allow one minute of quiet reflection and then proceed to Check-In.

0:05 CHECK-IN (20 MINUTES)

Let's begin our Check-In. Each person has two to three minutes to share her thoughts on the following topics:

- ☐ Status of your commitment.
- ☐ Your Growth Buddy connection: how was it, what worked, and any suggestions to enhance the connection.
- ☐ What I've learned about myself since our last session is . . .

Who would like to begin?

Remember that the Group Guide will model the time frame for Check-In. Tell the group that you'll be using the timer and that when the two minutes are up, the next person to her right checks in. Make sure you stay within the two-minute time frame. As each individual completes her Check-In, she lights a candle and states her intention for the session. After Check-In is completed, proceed to the next activity.

0:25 INTRODUCTION TO SEASONS OF MY LIFE (5 MINUTES)

Today's session is Seasons of My Life. This session will connect the group with one another by providing a structured activity designed to share our life stories, lessons learned, and experiences. The activity offers a concentrated autobiography for each of us. It is useful as a tool for understanding the past experiences, accomplishments, difficult times, and significant events in each of our lives.

0:30 SESSION ACTIVITY
SEASONS OF MY LIFE (1:40 MINUTES)

Divide the allotted time by the number of women in the group. This will give you the amount of time available for each woman. For example: if you have eight women in the group, divide 1 hour 40 minutes (i.e. 100 minutes) into eight segments. Each person thus has approximately 12 minutes.

Instruct the group to take out completed Session Accelerator 3.1: Seasons of My Life.

Each person has approximately *(number)* minutes to share her Seasons of My Life with the group. I'll set the digital timer for each woman. I'll give you a two-minute warning before the end of your allotted time so you can finish up your thoughts. Here are a few guidelines for this activity.

As a listener, pay attention to any themes, patterns, and specific language used by the speaker in describing her life. Also, be aware of any feelings or sensations that you notice in your body as you are listening deeply to the speaker's story.

As the speaker, pay attention to your sensations, feelings, and breathing. Speak your story from your heart, not your head. When one speaker has finished, we'll move immediately to the next speaker, and I'll reset the digital timer so that the next speaker can begin sharing her Seasons chart. This is not a time to ask questions, provide feedback, or give advice. It's a time to become aware of the wisdom and depth of experience each of us brings to our group. The person with the smallest feet goes first.

When half of the group has completed their Seasons timeline, I suggest taking a quick stretch break. This gives everyone a chance to move around a bit and refocus for the last half of the session.

After the last woman has shared her life story, tell the group that they'll have a few minutes to capture their thoughts about this activity.

2:10 CAPTURING WHAT MATTERS MOST TO ME (5 MINUTES)
Distribute Handout 3.1

We'll spend the next five minutes in silence to capture our thoughts and feelings about this session. Please take out your personal journal or use the handout to capture what matters most from today's session.

As you journal about this session, you might ask yourself:

- [ ] What decisions did you make about yourself and/or your life based on the events you shared?
- [ ] How do these decisions impact your life today?
- [ ] What was most valuable to you in this session?
- [ ] How are you feeling in this moment?

I'll be the timekeeper and set the digital timer for five minutes.

When time is up, you might ask:
Would anyone like to share one of her comments with the group?

Take a minute or two to listen to a few comments, and then continue on to the next activity.

2:15 MY COMMITMENTS (5 MINUTES)
Distribute Handout 3.2

We all have things in our life that we think about doing and haven't done, or have started and not completed. These *incompletes* drain energy from us and can keep us stuck in some areas of our lives. What incompletes in your life will you eliminate between now and the next time we meet? Take a moment and write on your commitment handout what incomplete you will finish or let go of between now and our next session. After everyone has finished writing we will read our commitments out loud to the group.

After everyone has written their commitments, say:
We'll take a few minutes now to share our commitments with each other. Begin by stating your commitment and why it is important to you at this time in your life.

Who would like to go first?

After the last woman has shared her commitments, thank the group and proceed to the Closing Circle.

2:20 CLOSING CIRCLE (5 MINUTES)
As we come to the end of this session, let's stand and form a circle. Take a moment to think of a word or brief thought that expresses what you experienced in the Seasons of My Life session.

Rotating around the Circle, each woman shares her word or thoughts. After everyone has shared in Closing Circle say:
This session is complete. Please extinguish your candle until we connect again.

2:25 WHAT'S NEXT—CALLING ON PURPOSE (5 MINUTES)
Ask for a volunteer to be the Group Guide for the next session. Remind the group that each group member will take on the role of Group Guide at least once during the next eight sessions. Invite everyone to take out her calendar and find a date that is available for the next session.

Our next session will be hosted by *(Group Guide's name)*, on *(date)*, at *(Group Guide's home)*, beginning promptly at *(time)*.

Calling on Purpose will be our topic. In order to prepare for this session and maximize our time together, the Session Accelerator: Excavating Purpose needs to be completed in advance. This Accelerator will take approximately one hour to complete. Please bring a copy of your completed Session Accelerator for each member of the group. *(Pass out Session Accelerator 4.1.)*

Choose a new Growth Buddy and decide when you will be connecting for the first time.

Afterthoughts

It is an incredible gift to have the opportunity to listen deeply to the life stories of the members in your Women Connected Group. I imagine that you heard similarities in some of the themes of one another's lives, as well as great differences. Often the realization occurs that we are all truly interconnected, and that, as I once remember reading, "everything and everyone is related to everything and everyone else." By now a feeling of trust is beginning to build within the group, and an inner knowing that each woman possesses a vast quantity of wisdom and experience to offer your group.

As you prepare for your next session, keep in mind your intention to follow the agreed upon Connecting Principles. If you believe that things are getting off track within the group, take it upon yourself to bring your concern forward within the group setting. This is a natural part of the Storming phase of your group's development process. The group will become stronger as it works through issues and each woman feels safe enough to express her views without fear of judgment. Rock and roll star Janis Joplin once said, "Don't compromise yourself. You are all you've got."

In our next session, Calling on Purpose, we'll consider all that we learned by looking at the seasons of our lives, and craft those learnings into our life purpose. In clarifying our sense of purpose, we'll be taking the first step toward the life we want to create—the life of our dreams.

Real change begins with the simple act of people
talking about what they care about.

□ MARGARET J. WHEATLEY

Handout 3.1

CAPTURING WHAT MATTERS MOST TO ME

☐ What decisions did you make about yourself and/or your life based on the events you shared?

☐ How do these decisions impact your life today?

☐ What was most valuable to you in this session?

☐ How are you feeling in this moment?

Handout 3.2

MY COMMITMENTS

Studies indicate that the one quality all successful
people have is persistence. They're willing
to spend more time accomplishing a task and to
persevere in the face of many difficult odds.

☐ DR. JOYCE BROTHERS

Today's Date _____

Commitment _____
_____
_____

Date completed _____

Commitment _____
_____
_____

Date completed _____

Commitment _____
_____
_____

Date completed _____

Session Accelerator 4.1
EXCAVATING PURPOSE

Create four symbols or pictures that represent your deepest, most cherished values.

Number these symbols or pictures in order of importance (1 being the most important, 2 the next most, and so on), and then answer the following questions about each symbol, in numerical order.

Use short phrases or words to complete the following:

- ☐ Who am I? *(Assume someone is genuinely interested in knowing who you are and she asks you to answer this question. Share the qualities that you love about yourself.)*
- ☐ Bring to mind your happiest moment or experience, or your greatest achievement. Describe how you were "being" in that moment. What traits or qualities were present?
- ☐ What most excites me about the world?
- ☐ If I could teach three things to others about what excites me in the world, what would I teach?
- ☐ What five things do I do that bring me great joy?
- ☐ The motto I do my best to live by.
- ☐ Qualities and traits: How I would like people to describe me if I died today.

Calling on

Purpose

I couldn't not do it . . . I'm programmed to make music.

☐ CARLY SIMON

When I listen to my heart, what does it say? What is the message? What am I destined to do while I live, breathe, play and work, and love others on this planet? What is my contribution? What is my legacy? What are my gifts, and how do I take those gifts out into the world? Without identifying my purpose, my calling, the reason that I get out of bed in the morning, I will wander aimlessly through life, without direction. Without a defined purpose, I may make choices in the moment without thinking about their long-term impact, or choices that keep my life small.

Choices made without a connection to purpose are not the kinds of choices that build a lasting legacy or provide a foundation for our gifts to make their way effectively into the world. As a result we may experience the results of choices that are not strategic, not connected to something larger than ourselves, and not intentional. For these reasons, it is critical that we spend time on this question: What is my purpose?

Several years ago I attended a workshop that was designed to look deeply into this question of purpose. After three days of experiential activities, I was in turmoil because I couldn't figure out my purpose. It was Saturday night, and on Sunday morning I was supposed to present My Purpose to the group, along with the steps I would take to align my life with that purpose. I wanted it to be perfect, I wanted it to sound important, and I wanted it to resonate with everyone in the room. At about 10 PM on Saturday night, I heard myself lamenting that I was a woman without a purpose! I had placed so much importance on finding the right words that I became stuck in the crafting of the purpose statement. I felt tense, tight, and overwhelmed.

It was at this moment that I asked for help. I asked my husband, Blaine, what he thought my purpose was. He laughed, "Your life purpose is so obvious to everyone!" (Oh great, I thought, everyone knows my purpose except me!) He went on, "You're all about connections! Everything you do is influenced by that. In your professional life you coach and train people to connect with their own internal wisdom, helping them to deepen their self-awareness, and

you absolutely love connecting people with resources that will support them in their life journey." When he said the word *connecting*, I knew that was it. At that moment my purpose was so obvious that I got chills! It was true: I couldn't imagine going through life *without making connections*. Whenever I'm expressing my purpose, I feel energized, excited, and passionate. The times in my life when I have been lonely, sad, bored, or semi-depressed, I was not acting on or from my purpose. Those have been the times when I felt disconnected from myself, disconnected from others, and disconnected from my life—because I was disconnected from my purpose. Like Carly Simon, I can't not do it . . . I'm programmed to connect.

This session provides the foundation you'll need to create a life of purpose, meaning, and personal fulfillment.

Words of Wisdom
FEELING STUCK?

There will be lots of clues as to what your purpose is in the Session Accelerator: Excavating Purpose. What words, phrases, or adjectives are you inclined to select in describing yourself? Look beneath these words and explore your feelings. What can you "not do"? Review the Seasons of Your Life timeline. Pay attention to themes that seem to emerge. What have you been drawn to during your life? Notice the big picture. Look at the patterns.

DO SOME RESEARCH

Ask a close friend what she or he thinks your purpose might be. Often others can see us more clearly than we can see ourselves. Pay attention to sensations and feelings; the more heat and energy, the more compelling and exciting a purpose.

REVIEW PURPOSE VERBS

Before you begin to write your Purpose Statement, spend time looking at Handout 4.2, Purpose Verbs, provided at the end of this chapter. They will help you bring your purpose to life.

Bumps in the Road—With Solutions!

INTERRUPTION OF SPEAKER

You have an *aha!* moment while another woman speaks about her purpose and, excited, you interrupt the speaker.

Solution: Express your regret and ponder whether you'd like to share with her after the session. In general, practice allowing a minute or two of silence before you speak, and ask the woman who is speaking if she is complete before you begin.

UNSOLICITED ADVICE

Because we care so much about purpose,

maybe you notice yourself or others giving advice to a group member when it has not been requested.

Solution: Ask questions rather than stating opinions. It's much more effective for a person to discover the answer within herself than to have others tell her what they think she should do.

IS MY PURPOSE GOOD ENOUGH?

You notice that you are comparing your purpose to the Purpose Statements of others.

Solution: This is an extremely tough one for us perfectionists! If you genuinely feel that energy and excitement has been generated for you from someone else's purpose, and it expresses more closely what you believe your purpose is, it's okay to make it your own.

SUPERFICIAL CONVERSATIONS

Conversations seem to be superficial and not as deep as you think they should be.

Solution: Remember that your group is still in the trust-building stage, and the more open you are, the more willing others will be to be authentic. Be a model of what you want from your group's members.

Sonia's Story

A witty woman with dark brown eyes and thick, naturally curly hair, Sonia possesses a great combination of intensity and warmth. Extremely loyal to family and friends, she is the kind of woman you can call in the middle of the night and she'll head for your doorstep without a moment's hesitation. Life hasn't been easy for Sonia; she has worked hard all her life and strives to be the best at whatever she takes on.

After completing a four-year degree in psychology, Sonia got a job at a well-known massage school. Her task was to enroll students, network in the community, and market the programs the school offered. Each day Sonia would watch the students coming out of class, hear their conversations, and engage them in dialogue about what they were learning. Mostly she noticed how happy and fulfilled they seemed, and she felt envious of their ability to really make a difference in the lives of their clients. Initially Sonia enjoyed her marketing job with its flexible hours, generous salary, and benefits. But something was missing. She often felt that there was another path she should be taking, and she shared with her Women Connected group that she just didn't know where to look. For Sonia, the Calling on Purpose session was life-changing. She had never spent time considering her life purpose or the implications of working in a profession that was not in alignment with her calling. In defining her purpose—To Be a Creative Healer—it became clear that Sonia needed to make some changes at work and in her life.

As the months went by, Sonia felt less and less interested in her job, but she couldn't afford to quit. Then one day something within her clicked. She decided to ask her boss if she could rearrange her schedule so that she could attend massage school full time. Once Sonia began to attend classes, she knew she was finally in the right place. Even though she was working long hours, her desired end result was in sight: a degree in massage therapy, and the opportunity to be aligned with her purpose and her vision of owning a business. Today Sonia owns a thriving massage therapy business, and she has doubled her income since leaving her marketing job at the massage school.

The Big Picture: Calling on Purpose

Suggested Time Frames	Activity	Purpose	Materials | Set-up
:05	Opening	Welcome; transition into Women Connected; become present	• Poem
:20	Check-In	Update, reconnect, report	• Candle for each woman
1:45	Session: Calling on Purpose	Write a Purpose Statement, which will be the guiding principle in creating a life connected to your highest, best self	• Completed Session Accelerator 4.1 Excavating Purpose • Handout 4.1 My Purpose • Handout 4.2 Purpose Verbs • Handout 4.3 Composing Your Purpose
.03 (per person)	Wisdom Blast	Access the group's wisdom	• Handout 4.4 Wisdom Blast • Paper and pen • Scribe • Timekeeper
:05	Capturing What Matters Most to Me	Highlight session insights that are most relevant to your life	• Personal journal or Handout 4.5 Capturing What Matters Most to Me
:05	My Commitments	Increase accountability, intention, and likelihood of successful goal attainment	• Handout 4.6 My Commitments
:05	Closing Circle	Complete the session	• Standing circle • Extinguish candles
:05	Logistics for next session	Ensure Group continuity and clarity of requirements for the next session	• Designate Group Guide, time, place • Choose a new Growth Buddy • Session Accelerator 5.1 My Purpose

What Happens During the "Calling on Purpose" Session

0:00 WELCOME (5 MINUTES)

Prior to starting the group, place a candle for each woman near the location where the group will be gathered. Each woman will light a candle at the completion of her Check-In.

Group Guide welcomes the group to her home and this session.

Inform the group that there will be a couple of minutes of silence. The purpose is to quiet the mind, get present, and shift focus to intentional conversations.

Begin by taking three or four deep breaths. As you inhale, breathe deeply into all the possibilities waiting to be discovered. As you exhale, sink deeply into your authentic self and relax into a state of openness and connection to self, becoming present to new possibilities. Elisabeth Kubler-Ross said "Learn to get in touch with the silence within yourself, and know that everything in this life has a purpose."

Group Guide reads her preselected poem.
After the poem is read say:
Silently affirm to yourself the intention you're holding for this session. How will you show up in today's session, what will you contribute, and how will you demon-

What You'll Need
- Poem
- Candle for each woman
- Digital timer
- Personal journal or notebook
- Calendar for setting next session's date
- Session Accelerator 4.1 Excavating Purpose
- Handout 4.1 My Purpose
- Handout 4.2 Purpose Verbs
- Handout 4.3 Composing Your Purpose
- Handout 4.4 Wisdom Blast
- Handout 4.5 Capturing What Matters Most to Me
- Handout 4.6 My Commitments
- Session Accelerator 5.1 My Purpose

Session Accelerator and handouts are provided as downloadable files at www.WomenConnected.com

strate your support to the group?

Allow one minute of quiet reflection, and then proceed to Check-In.

0:05 CHECK-IN (20 MINUTES)

Let's begin our Check-In. Each person has two to three minutes to share her thoughts on the following topics:

☐ Report the status of your last session's commitment.

☐ Describe your Growth Buddy connection: how was it, what worked, and any suggestions to enhance the connection.

☐ What I learned about myself since last session is . . .

Who would like to begin?

Remember that the Group Guide will model the time frame for Check-In. Tell the group that you'll be using the digital timer and that when the two minutes are up, the next person to her right checks in. Make certain that you stay within the two-minute time frame.

As each individual completes her Check-In, she lights a candle and states her intention for the session.

After Check-In is complete, proceed to the next activity.

0:25 INTRODUCTION TO CALLING ON PURPOSE (5 MINUTES)

Today's session is Calling on Purpose. The focus of this session is to craft a statement that reflects your life purpose. This is one of the most critical steps in creating a life of meaning and personal fulfillment. Purpose acts as our inner compass and supports us in orienting our life's work. *Purpose* has been defined in many ways throughout history. Here are some definitions of *purpose*.

☐ Our reason for being.
☐ The reason for getting up in the morning.
☐ The source of energy and direction.
☐ What fuels us.
☐ The quality we choose to create our lives around.
☐ Our natural desire to contribute to life.
☐ When our heart's desire and the needs of the world come together.

0:30 LISTENING FOR PURPOSE (45 MINUTES)

Instruct group to take out completed Session Accelerator 4.1

During the first part of our session, we will be sharing our responses from the Session Accelerator: Excavating Purpose. As you listen to each woman, notice if you can pick up any clues that provide insight into her life purpose. Do there seem to be recurring themes or certain adjectives that she uses to describe her experiences? Quite possibly you might be the one to assist her in defining and being able to see her life purpose.

If your group has five or fewer members, I suggest the entire group share their responses as one group. With five women, you'll have eight minutes per person. With a larger group I suggest dividing the group in half. This will give each woman more time to share her responses and allow time for any questions that the others in the group might have for her. Assign a timekeeper for the second group.

We have approximately 40 minutes to complete this activity. I will act as the timekeeper in my group. Let's begin.

At the completion of 40 minutes, say:
Sometimes we discover that what gives our lives purpose and meaning is not what we originally expected. As we go forward, we'll be learning even more about ourselves.

1:15 CRAFTING PURPOSE STATEMENTS (30 MINUTES)

It's now time for the second part of the purpose activity. Pair up with your Growth Buddy and then I'll lead everyone through the directions for crafting our Purpose Statements.

Pause for a minute until everyone is settled.

We'll have 30 minutes to complete a draft of our Purpose Statements.

If your Growth Buddy gets stuck in this process, you'll ask her questions to elicit her inner wisdom. This is a great place to practice your coaching skills! To assist you in the process, here are a few examples of Purpose Statements:

- ☐ My purpose is to create environments where people connect deeply with themselves and others in magnificent and powerful ways.
- ☐ My purpose is to be a positive influence on the lives of my children.
- ☐ My purpose is to make my community—the places where I live and work—more healthy and beautiful.
- ☐ My purpose is to teach love, inspire hope, and create healing in others and myself.
- ☐ My purpose is to dare to be true, to be courageous, and to believe in what I want.
- ☐ My purpose is to live a life of faith and creative spirit, to impart change, and to heal myself and others through living with intent and purpose.

Distribute Handout 4.1: My Purpose, Handout 4.2: Purpose Verbs, and Handout 4.3: Composing Your Purpose

The Purpose Verbs will assist you in finding words that best reflect your purpose. It is to be used as a guide and resource for the crafting of your statement.

While creating your Purpose Statement, it is important to express your purpose in the present tense. Plan to spend 15 minutes per person on this activity. I'll set the timer for 15 minutes so we'll know when to switch speakers. Then I'll reset the timer for the last 15 minutes of the activity. Please begin.

After 30 minutes has passed, tell the group that the time is up and invite them to come back together in a large circle.

1:45 SHARING OUR PURPOSES (10 MINUTES)

Let's gather together and share our Purpose Statements. Remember that they don't need to be perfect. This is our first draft. Our completed Purpose Statements will be brought to our next session. I'll go first, and we'll continue around the circle until everyone has read her Purpose Statement.

Before reading the Purpose Statements, tell the group that if anyone needs extra help, there is a Women Connected process called the Wisdom Blast that will assist her. Group Guide reads her Purpose Statement, and the person on her right goes next. Continue around the circle until everyone has read her Purpose Statement.

We have time for three or four people to participate in a Wisdom Blast. This is a process of structured brainstorming that will generate additional ideas to help you write out your purpose.

1:55 WISDOM BLAST (15 MINUTES)
Distribute Handout 4.4

The Wisdom Blast is a process designed to access the wisdom of the group. For three minutes we'll generate as many ideas as possible for each woman who wants assistance on answering the question: What is my purpose?

A quick formula for determining how much time the group has for a Wisdom Blast is this: Check the current time, subtract 20 minutes (the suggested time left for the remainder of the entire session), and see how many minutes you have left for this activity. If you have six minutes, there is time for two women to have a Wisdom Blast, based on three minutes per person. The group always has the option to extend the session if everyone agrees and can stay until the end.

With the time left in today's session, we're able to have *(number)* women participate in this process. Who would like to experience a Wisdom Blast today?

If more women want to participate than the group has time for, I suggest having all the interested women pick a number between 1 and 25. The women with numbers closest to the number pre-selected by the Group Guide will experience the Wisdom Blast. To ease any disappointment, remind the group that there will be more Wisdom Blast opportunities in the future.

During the Wisdom Blast everyone has permission to give advice freely. All of our ideas will be written down and given to the woman at the center of the Wisdom Blast. Later she'll e-mail the group members (or check-in at the following session) to share what she did with our amazing advice. Who would like to write down the advice that is given during this Wisdom Blast? *(Wait for someone to volunteer.)* Let's begin.

The Group Guide will set digital timer for three minutes per person. Once three minutes are up, quickly move to the next person. It is the Group Guide's responsibility to keep the Wisdom Blast moving and to watch the time. If the Group Guide wants to participate in the Wisdom Blast, she should pass these responsibilities on to someone else.

When the Wisdom Blast process is complete, thank the group for their fabulous advice and proceed to Capturing What Matters Most.

2:10 CAPTURING WHAT MATTERS MOST TO ME (5 MINUTES)
Distribute Handout 4.5

We'll spend the next five minutes in silence to capture our thoughts and feelings about this session. Please take out your personal journal or use the handout to capture what matters most from today's session.

As you journal about this session, you might ask yourself:
- ☐ What was most valuable to me in this session?
- ☐ How did it feel to be supported in drafting my purpose statement?

☐   How did it feel to support my Growth Buddy in drafting her purpose statement?

I'll be the timekeeper and set the digital timer for five minutes.

When time is up, you might ask: Would anyone like to share one of her comments with the group?

Take a minute or two, listen to a few comments, and then continue on to the next activity.

2:15 MY COMMITMENTS (5 MINUTES)
Distribute Handout 4.6

Take a moment to decide what you'd like to commit to between now and our next session. It is useful to think of a commitment that is aligned with your purpose. For example, if my purpose is to create peace in my community, my commitment might be to introduce myself to a new neighbor, or to volunteer for a day at an elementary school.

After everyone has written her commitments, say:
We'll take a few minutes now and share our commitments with each other. Begin by stating your commitment and why it's important to you at this time in your life. Who'd like to go first?

After the last woman has shared her commitments, thank the group and proceed to the Closing Circle.

2:20 CLOSING CIRCLE (5 MINUTES)
As we come to the end of this session, let's stand and form a circle. Take a moment to think of a word or brief thought that expresses what you experienced in the Calling on Purpose session.

Rotating around the Circle, each woman shares her word or thoughts. After everyone has shared in Closing Circle, say:

This session is complete. Please extinguish your candle until we connect again.

2:25 WHAT'S NEXT—FUTURE PERFECT (5 MINUTES)

Ask for a volunteer to be the Group Guide for the next session. Remind the group that each group member will take on the role of Group Guide at least once during the next seven sessions. Instruct everyone to take out her calendar to find an available date for the next session.

Our next session will be hosted by *(Group Guide's name)*, on *(date)*, at *(Group Guide's home)*, beginning promptly at *(time)*.

Future Perfect is the focus of our next session. In order to prepare for this session and maximize our time together, the Session Accelerator: My Purpose needs to be completed in advance. Please bring copies of your completed Purpose Statement for each member of the group. This is the Session Accelerator for the next session. *(Pass out Session Accelerator 5.1.)*

Choose a new Growth Buddy and decide when you will be connecting for the first time.

Afterthoughts

This session has focused on defining and writing your Purpose Statement. It may be that you were able to finish your Purpose Statement. More often than not, however, additional work and time for reflection are needed to complete this important assignment.

For assistance you might ask a friend or a significant other what words they would use to describe you at your best. Your Growth Buddy is a great resource, too. Remember that the Purpose Statement doesn't have to be perfect; it can and probably will be a work in progress. The question

"What is my purpose?" isn't to be answered in a hurry; it's a question to live with. Try on your answers and adjust them over time. You will eventually find just the right words to express your purpose.

Calling on Purpose has been about looking inward. The next session, Future Perfect, is designed to look outward. It's a fun and exciting session, and it's one of my favorites. It's practically impossible not to get excited about expanding your imagination and thinking really big thoughts about your future! The Women Connected train has definitely left the station. Hold on tight—here we go!

You must first be who you really are, then do what
    you need to do, in order to have what you want.

□ MARGARET YOUNG

Handout 4.1

MY PURPOSE

Handout 4.2

PURPOSE VERBS

Below is a list of verbs. Pick out the three verbs from each column that most excite you. Then select the Ultimate Three. These are the action words that will shape your Purpose Statement.

accomplish	compliment	embrace	heal	mold	reduce	support
acquire	compose	encourage	hold	motivate	refine	surrender
adopt	conceive	endow	host	move	reflect	sustain
advance	confirm	engage	identify	negotiate	reform	take
affect	connect	engineer	illuminate	nurture	regard	tap
affirm	consider	enhance	implement	open	relate	team
alleviate	construct	enlighten	improve	organize	relax	touch
amplify	contact	enlist	improvise	participate	release	trade
appreciate	continue	enliven	inspire	pass	rely	translate
ascend	counsel	entertain	integrate	perform	remember	travel
associate	create	enthuse	involve	persuade	renew	understand
believe	decide	evaluate	keep	play	resonate	use
bestow	defend	excite	know	possess	respect	utilize
brighten	delight	explore	labor	practice	restore	validate
build	deliver	express	launch	praise	return	value
call	demonstrate	extend	lead	prepare	revise	venture
cause	devise	facilitate	light	present	sacrifice	verbalize
choose	direct	finance	live	produce	safeguard	volunteer
claim	discover	forgive	love	progress	satisfy	work
collect	discuss	foster	make	promise	save	worship
combine	distribute	franchise	manifest	promote	sell	write
command	draft	further	master	provide	serve	yield
communicate	dream	gather	mature	pursue	share	
compel	drive	generate	measure	realize	speak	
compete	educate	give	mediate	receive	stand	
complete	elect	grant	model	reclaim	summon	

Handout 4.3

COMPOSING YOUR PURPOSE—IDEA GENERATING ACTIVITIES

☐ Write down your three most meaningful, purposeful, and exciting verbs.

☐ Explore what principle, cause, value, or purpose you would be willing to take a stand for, or devote your life to.

☐ Ask significant people in your life about what you are doing or how you are being, when you seem most alive and energized.

☐ Ask your group for a Wisdom Blast.

Handout 4.4
WISDOM BLAST

This is a process designed to access the group's collective wisdom. It is a brainstorming session, and any idea is worth listening to. Sometimes the best ideas come out of left field! Each woman has the option to bring an issue, challenge, or dilemma before the group. For three minutes, the group generates as many ideas as possible to help address the issue. This is the only time when giving advice is encouraged.

The role of the group is to stay focused, with the intention of providing solutions to the problem described. The role of the recipient is to listen, without comment or judgments. Just stay present, focused, and open to receiving the wisdom from the group.

The recipient's Growth Buddy will capture all ideas generated by the group. Before the next session, look over this list and choose what you believe to be the best solution. Try out the solution and report back to the group during the next Check-In.

Handout 4.5

CAPTURING WHAT MATTERS MOST TO ME

☐   What was most valuable to you in this session?

☐   How did it feel to be supported in drafting your purpose statement?

☐   How did it feel to support your Growth Buddy in drafting her purpose
     statement?

Handout 4.6

MY COMMITMENTS

Whoever said anybody has the right to quit? You are *not* obligated to win, you're obligated to keep trying to do the best you can every day.

☐ MARIAN WRIGHT EDELMAN

Today's Date _____

Commitment _____

_____

_____

Date completed _____

Commitment _____

_____

_____

Date completed _____

Commitment _____

_____

_____

Date completed _____

Session Accelerator 5.1

MY PURPOSE

Bring a copy of your Purpose Statement for each woman in the group.

Future

Perfect

Ask yourself what dreams a person with your life purpose would want. Then listen for the answers.

☐ MARCIA WIEDER

Many of the people who knew me growing up would be surprised to see the life I'm living today: a life blessed with healthy relationships, abundance, and beauty; fulfillment in many shapes and forms. Even when things appeared grim on the outside, some part of me always believed that things could (and would) steadily improve in my life. I set out with the intention to help those things happen, and I had support in doing it. If I hadn't made conscious commitments to my Women Connected coaching group, and if I hadn't experienced their unconditional faith in me, I wouldn't be where I am today. Great news: I know this process that has worked so well for me can work equally well for you.

In over 15 years of working with Women Connected coaching groups, I've encountered quite a few women who spoke with enthusiasm about making their dreams a reality, but for whom, in the end, it came to no more than talk. For most, however, their personal accountability, their commitment, and the support of their Women Connected group have made their cherished dreams come true. This session has the power to set you on the road to transformation.

When I was a little girl, there was a TV show called "The Millionaire." Each week we watched as the Millionaire (who remained anonymous) selected a new person to give a million dollars to, with no strings attached. After each show my sister, Penny, and I would make lists of all the things we would buy if we had a million dollars. My mother always got a fur coat, we got a house with bedrooms of our own, and, of course, we bought a brand new red car. As Penny and I got older, we continued to play the million dollar game on car trips and vacations. After I married and had children of my own, we continued to play the million dollar game, making our lists and believing that our future dreams would come true.

Some of those lists are stored in my memory boxes—written proof that Future Perfect is real. The yacht I wanted became a 46-foot sailboat; the large mansion with a swimming pool (a wish held when I was 11 years old) turned up as a big house with a hot tub; and when my grandma passed away my mother inherited the fur coat I

had wished for her. A great many of the dreams on my million dollar list have come true, and I believe this is because I dreamed big and stuck with my vivid imagining of a better and brighter future.

The way to begin to change your life is to describe the life you want without needing to know *how* it will happen. For your dreams to come true, it's important to think big, without limitations, and to speak your dreams out loud to others—to your Women Connected group. The way you describe your future world profoundly influences what shows up in your life.

In this session you'll have the opportunity to describe your future, exactly the way you want it to be. You'll put the details of your future life into words and share the richness of your Future Perfect with your Women Connected group.

Let your imagination run wild! It's crucial to avoid censoring yourself. We all know how to be practical; the challenge and fun is to be childlike and allow our imaginations to soar. Truly *believe* that you can have a Future Perfect. Now is the time to ask for everything you want and to believe that everything is possible. You've got nothing to lose and a Future Perfect to gain.

Words of Wisdom

ROTATING PARTNERS

The Future Perfect activity is designed to be done with partners. If there is an odd number of women in your group, arrange for one group to consist of three women. Rotate after each round, so that everyone has an opportunity to be in a group of three at least once.

LET YOUR IDEAS FLOW FREELY

If you get stuck, keep talking. Remember that you can adopt the ideas of others. This is what collaboration and Women Connected is all about: supporting each other, being resources for one another, and being there for yourself as well, as you make your future dreams come true.

Bumps in the Road—With Solutions!

HITTING THE IMAGINARY WALL

Every now and then a woman will have difficulty even *imagining* a life without bounds, a life in which almost anything is possible.

Solution: Remind yourself that unless you try something different, your life will continue to look the same. Take a deep breath and say to yourself, *I'm worth it, and I'm going to give this a try!*

CHANGING THE CHANNEL

A voice in your head may be saying, *This is silly. What does this have to do with goal setting? I don't want to share crazy ideas that won't come true! If I share something, does it mean I have to follow through?*

Solution: Notice what you're saying to yourself, acknowledge it, and then make a conscious decision to change the message. We all have several voices in our heads. You can think of these voices as different stations on the radio. When it's a think-small voice that makes you wrong, consciously decide to switch to a station that supports your growth, success, and future motion in creating the life you so richly deserve.

IF THE WORD PERFECT GETS IN YOUR WAY

You may be thinking, *nothing is ever perfect. How can I ever reach perfection? Who am I to think I can have things exactly as I want them?*

Solution: Rather than being concerned about perfectionism or the word *perfect*, you can simply try acting as if anything is possible. What would it look like if your life were just as you liked it? If an ordinary life would make you happiest, what are the features of that ordinary life? Imagine that you have all the wisdom and resources you need to move your future forward successfully.

NOT ENOUGH TIME

This activity is a lot of fun. It's extremely energizing, and time tends to get away from you. A common complaint, especially in this session, is *There wasn't enough time, I felt hurried, I was just warming up, and I'm not a quick thinker.*

Solution: It's important to have group agreement about being on time, starting sessions on time, and ending at an agreed-upon time. You'll need to help each other to be succinct with your sharing, reminding each other about getting to the heart of the matter rather than sharing all of the details leading up to your experience.

Deanna's Story

When she smiles, which is often, her greenish blue eyes narrow to the shape of a crescent moon and almost disappear. Sensitive to the needs of others, Deanna is usually the first in her group to notice if someone is having a tough day. She is thoughtful and caring, with a big heart that opens up readily to those in need. Deanna doesn't hesitate if she is asked to help a friend, and gives away her time without regrets. Helping others get what they want in life and supporting their dreams makes her happy. More often than not, her own dreams have been kept on hold, and her follow-though has been, in her words, "almost nonexistent."

The Future Perfect session couldn't have come at a better time in Deanna's life. She seemed at loose ends, working at a dead-end job, single, uncertain of her future, and she described her finances as "in the toilet." During this Women Connected session, she expanded her thinking in a direction that seemed almost impossible to attain. Deanna shared her future dreams of being happily married, financially secure, in a job that was challenging, physically fit and wearing a size 4, and she wanted to have children. At the time it all seemed possible, but based on her past it was highly improbable. Yet, her Women Connected friends knew that she could have it all, and more. They were her cheerleaders and guides, and they held her accountable for following through with her dreams.

Today Deanna's life is much different than it was five years ago. She has been happily married to Todd for three years, is the mother of an adorable baby named Oliver, works in a job that she loves, has a 401k plan, owns a home, and has decided that being a size 8 is just fine!

The Big Picture: Future Perfect

Suggested Time Frames	Activity	Purpose	Materials | Set-up
:05	Opening	Welcome; transition into Women Connected; become present	▪ Poem
:30	Check-In	Update, reconnect, report	▪ Candle for each woman ▪ Completed Session Accelerator 5.1 My Purpose
1:20	Session: Future Perfect	Generate excitement and open yourself up to a life bigger than you dreamed was possible	▪ Group Guide will be timekeeper ▪ Handout 5.1 Future Perfect Notes
:15	Capturing What Matters Most to Me	Highlight session insights that are most relevant to your life	▪ Personal journal or Handout 5.2 Capturing What Matters Most to Me
:10	My Commitments	Increase accountability, intention, and likelihood of successful goal attainment	▪ Handout 5.3 My Commitments
:05	Closing Circle	Complete the session	▪ Standing circle ▪ Extinguish candles
:05	Logistics for next session	Ensure Group continuity and clarity of requirements for the next session	▪ Designate Group Guide, time, place ▪ Choose a new Growth Buddy ▪ Handout 5.4 Sample Vision Statements ▪ Session Accelerator 6.1 Women Connected Tune-Up ▪ Session Accelerator 6.2 My Vision

What You'll Need

- Poem
- Candle for each woman
- Digital timer
- Personal journal or notebook
- Calendar for setting next session's date
- Session Accelerator 5.1 My Purpose
- Handout 5.1 Future Perfect Notes
- Handout 5.2 Capturing What Matters Most to Me
- Handout 5.3 My Commitments
- Handout 5.4 Sample Vision Statements
- Session Accelerator 6.1 Women Connected Tune-Up
- Session Accelerator 6.2 My Vision

Session Accelerators and handouts are provided as downloadable files at www.WomenConnected.com

What Happens During the "Future Perfect" Session

0:00 WELCOME (5 MINUTES)

Prior to starting the group, place a candle for each woman near the location where the group will be gathered. Each woman will light a candle at the completion of her Check-In.

Welcome to my home and to this session: Future Perfect. I'm so happy you're here and I know that the work we'll do in this session is likely to be life-changing for each one of us. To begin, let's take a few moments to quiet our minds, to become present right here and now, and to shift our focus to our intention for this session. Please get into a comfortable position.

Allow a few moments for the women to get comfortable.

You may want to close your eyes to help eliminate any distractions. Now, begin by taking three or four deep breaths. As you inhale, breathe deeply into all the possibilities waiting to be discovered. As you exhale, sink deeply into your authentic self. Relax into a state of openness and connection to self, and become present to new possibilities.

Group Guide reads her preselected poem.
After the poem is read say:
Silently affirm to yourself the intention you're holding for this session. How will you show up for today's session, what will you contribute, and how will you demonstrate your support to the group?

Allow one minute of quiet reflection and then proceed to Check-In.

0:05 CHECK-IN (30 MINUTES)

Let's begin our Check-In. Each person has

three to four minutes to share her thoughts on the following topics:

- ☐ Begin by stating your purpose.
- ☐ Report the status of your last session's commitment.
- ☐ Describe your Growth Buddy connection—how was it, what worked, and any suggested tune-up.
- ☐ What I have learned about myself since our last session is . . .

Who would like to begin?

Remember that the Group Guide will model the time frame on Check-In. Tell the group that you'll be using the digital timer and that when three minutes are up, the next person to her right checks in. Be sure to stay within the three-minute time frame.

As each individual completes her Check-In, she lights a candle and states her intention for the session.

After Check-In is complete, proceed to the next activity.

0:35 INTRODUCTION TO FUTURE PERFECT (5 MINUTES)

Today's session is Future Perfect. The purpose of this session is to generate excitement about your life, to expand your choices, to help you think big thoughts, and to act as if everything you desire is possible.

0:40 IMAGERY (10 MINUTES)

I am going to lead you through a visualization process. Sometimes people find it difficult to visualize with their eyes closed. They tend to be more kinesthetic or sensation oriented, or more connected to their other senses, and that's just fine. If it's hard for you to visualize, engage your other senses in this visioning process. If you are comfortable with eyes closed, please shut your eyes and we will begin.

Take a deep, long breath, hold it *(pause 5 seconds)*, and slowly release. Take another breath and follow it through your nose, down into your lungs, hold it *(pause 10 seconds)*, and exhale. Now take a deeper breath, drawing the air in through your nose and down to fill your lungs completely, hold it *(pause 5 seconds)*, and exhale. . . . Imagine the tension and worries from the day flowing out with each breath you take *(pause 5 seconds)*. Notice the rhythm of your own breathing . . . let it set a rhythm for you; pace yourself with it *(pause 10 seconds)*.

As you breathe in, say silently to yourself "I am," and then silently say "relaxed" as you breathe out *(pause 10 seconds)*. Once again as you breathe in, say silently to yourself "I am," and then silently say "relaxed" as you breathe out *(pause 10 seconds)*.

In this relaxed and open state, I'd like you to imagine that it is one year from today. We have been meeting in our Women Connected coaching group for one year. It is a time of celebration. Together we have achieved our dreams and fulfilled our commitments, and our lives are exactly how we want them to be *(pause 5 seconds)*. Let your thoughts of our year together wash over you *(pause 10 seconds)*.

☐ Looking back over the year, what are you most proud of creating? *(pause 20 seconds)*
☐ What dreams did you make come true? *(pause 20 seconds)*
☐ What do your relationships look like? *(pause 20 seconds)*
☐ What have you achieved at work and at home? *(pause 20 seconds)*
☐ What is the state of your finances? *(pause 20 seconds)*
☐ How do you feel physically, emotionally, spiritually? *(pause 20 seconds)*

Take time to visualize how different your life looks than it did a year ago. Watch and listen to what happens as you silently share with your Women Connected group how your year has unfolded. *(pause 20 seconds)* If you notice any resistance coming up during the imagery, it's okay; just take a deep breath and be with whatever feelings come up. *(pause 2-3 minutes)*

In just a moment I'm going to ask you to open your eyes and rejoin the group, here, today, on *(today's date; pause)*. Please open your eyes. *(pause)* Let's take some time now to discuss this experience with one another.

0:50 IMAGERY—LARGE GROUP DISCUSSION (10 MINUTES)
☐ What was the imagery like for you?
☐ What did you see, what did you notice, how did it feel?

After a few people have shared their thoughts, say:
It's now time to begin the activity for today's session, Future Perfect.

1:00 FUTURE PERFECT NOTES (5 MINUTES)

Before beginning this activity, instruct the group to choose partners. If there are an odd number in the group, it's okay to have three people working together.

After everyone (including you) has found a partner, distribute Handout 5.1 and say:
This handout will be used by your partner to take notes on what you say during this activity. I suggest you record the key phrases and highlights that are shared; it is not necessary to record every word. Write your name and today's date on the handout.

There will be four rounds in this activity, and during each round you will have a different partner. I will set the digital timer for each round, and when the timer goes off, please be silent and wait for the next set of directions for each of the rounds.

From this point onward, imagine that it is one year from today. We have been magically transported into the future, and our lives are absolutely perfect in every way. Speak in present tense language, and act as if all your dreams have come true. It's okay to pretend. This is not the time to censor yourself or to be concerned with how you are going to accomplish your dreams. We can work on that next session. Just go for it and really let your imagination travel wherever it goes. This activity is designed to be fun and energizing, and to stir the creative juices in each of us. The more detailed you are, the more empowered you will be to create a result you desire.

- ☐ As you describe your life, some of the things will be things you've thought about for years.
- ☐ Some will be things you've never even dreamed of before.
- ☐ Knowing what you want determines what you will get.
- ☐ Before something happens in the world, it must first happen in your mind.

Now it's time to create our Future Perfect.

1:05 ROUND 1 FUTURE PERFECT ACTIVITY (10 MINUTES)
For all rounds, the Group Guide is responsible for monitoring the time.

The person with the shortest hair goes first. She will be Partner A. Partner B will listen and record A's responses to the Round 1 question. For your convenience, the questions for Round 1 are listed on your Future Perfect Notes Handout 5.1.

☐ You have five minutes to tell your partner all about your perfect life. It's ideal and perfect in every way!

☐ It's okay to borrow ideas. If you hear something that you would like to incorporate into your life, when it's your turn make it yours!

☐ If you run out of things to say, just start over.

☐ Remember to speak in present tense language.

☐ You're so excited about this, you almost can't stand it—your life is perfect!—so bring those emotions to your story.

The instructions for this round are as follows:

☐ Describe your ideal life (one year from today).

☐ What's going on?

☐ What does it feel like; what are you hearing, tasting, touching, and seeing?

☐ What's going on in your relationships, work, leisure time, finances, health, etc.

Partner A, give Partner B your Future Perfect Notes handout. Ready, begin.

Group Guide sets the digital timer for five minutes. After five minutes, the Group Guide says:
Time is up. Now it's time for Partner B to share her perfect life. Remember B, if you heard A say something you really liked, it's okay to use the idea and weave it into your perfect life. B, you'll give A your Future Perfect

Notes so she can record your responses. I'll tell you when the five minutes are up. Begin.

After five minutes, the Group Guide says: Time is up.

1:15 ROUND 2 (10 MINUTES)

Now it's time for Round 2. Please choose a different partner.

Wait until everyone has a new partner, then say:
The partner with the biggest feet goes first. You will be A.

- ☐ Partner B takes A's Future Perfect Notes and records her responses to the Round 2 question.
- ☐ Partner A starts at the beginning and shares her perfect life from Round 1, since this is a new partner who hasn't heard what has happened during the last year.
- ☐ As she tells her story, Partner A shares the major obstacles and fears she overcame during the year, to make this ideal life what it is today. Partner B records her responses.
- ☐ It's okay to borrow ideas, so build on what you hear if it fits for you.
- ☐ You have five minutes per person in this activity. Please begin.

Group Guide sets digital timer for five minutes. When the timer goes off, say:
Now it's time for Partner B to give A her Future Perfect Notes, so that she can record the responses. Please begin.

Group Guide sets digital timer for five minutes. After five minutes, the Group Guide says:
Time is up.

1:25 ROUND 3 (10 MINUTES)

Now it's time for Round 3. Please choose a different partner.

After everyone has found a new partner, say:

The partner with the most jewelry goes first. You will be A.

☐ Partner B takes Partner A's Future Perfect Notes and records her responses to the Round 3 question.

☐ Partner A starts at the beginning and shares her perfect life from Rounds 1 and 2, since this is a new partner who hasn't heard all the wonderful things that have happened during the last year.

☐ This time while telling her story, Partner A shares the key people and resources that were involved in making her dreams come true this year. Partner B records her responses.

☐ Remember, it is still okay to borrow ideas, so build on what you hear that fits for you.

You have five minutes per person for this activity.

Group Guide sets digital timer for five minutes. When the timer goes off, say:

Now it's time for Partner B to give A her Future Perfect Notes, so that she can record her responses. Please begin.

Group Guide sets digital timer for five minutes. After five minutes, the Group Guide says:

Time is up.

1:35 ROUND 4 (10 MINUTES)

We've reached Round 4, our last round. Please choose a different partner.

When everyone has found a new partner, say:

The partner who has the next birthday goes first! You will be A.

☐ Partner B takes Partner A's Future Perfect Notes and records her responses to the Round 4 question.

☐ This time Partner A starts at the beginning and shares her perfect life with a specific focus on what she is personally most proud of having created.

☐ Remember, it is still okay to borrow ideas, so build on what you hear that fits for you.

You have five minutes per person for this activity. This is where you really get excited: this is what you're most proud of!

Group Guide sets digital timer for five minutes. When the timer goes off, say:

Now it's time for Partner B to give A her Future Perfect Notes, so that she can record her responses. Please begin.

Group Guide sets digital timer for five minutes. After five minutes, the Group Guide says:
Our time is up. Let's get back together and discuss what we've experienced during this activity.

1:45 FUTURE PERFECT
LARGE GROUP DISCUSSION (10 MINUTES)
Group Guide leads a discussion with the group.

☐ What did you notice as you went through the different rounds?

☐ Did your vision change as you heard the ideas of others?

☐ What were your favorite rounds? How many of you started believing what you said?

When the discussion is complete, please proceed to the next activity.

1:55 CAPTURING WHAT MATTERS MOST TO ME (5 MINUTES)
Distribute Handout 5.2

We'll spend the next five minutes in silence to capture our thoughts and feelings about this session. Please take out your personal journal or use the handout to capture what matters most from today's session.

As you journal about this session you might ask yourself:

☐ What is it like to imagine a life that is perfect in every way?

☐ Were you able to act as if it was possible?

☐ How are you feeling in this moment?

I'll be the timekeeper and set the digital timer for five minutes.

2:00 CAPTURING WHAT MATTERS MOST
LARGE GROUP DISCUSSION (10 MINUTES)
Who would like to share her journal entry?

Take time to listen to the women share their points of view about Future Perfect. It is not necessary to make comments during this time, just make sure that whoever wants to speak has the opportunity.

When the sharing is complete, proceed to the next activity.

2:10 MY COMMITMENTS (10 MINUTES)
Distribute Handout 5.3

Take a moment and decide what you'd like to commit to between now and our next session. Think of a commitment that is aligned with creating your Future Perfect. It can be a small step that moves you in the direction of where you want to be at the end of one year.

After each woman has finished writing her commitments say the following:
We'll take a few minutes now to share our commitments with each other. Start by stating your commitment, and say why it is important to you at this time in your life. Who would like to go first?

After the last woman has shared her commitments, thank the group and proceed to the Closing Circle.

2:20 CLOSING CIRCLE (5 MINUTES)

As we come to the end of this session, let's stand and form a circle. Take a moment to think of a word or brief thought that expresses what you experienced today in the Future Perfect session.

Rotating around the Circle, each woman shares her word or thoughts. After everyone has shared in Closing Circle, say:
This session is complete. Please extinguish your candle until we connect again.

2:25 WHAT'S NEXT—DREAMS IN MOTION (5 MINUTES)

Ask for a volunteer to be the Group Guide for the next session. Remind the group that each group member will take on the role of Group Guide at least once during the remaining sessions. Instruct everyone to take out her calendar and find a date that is available for the next session.

Our next session will be hosted by *(Group Guide's name)*, on *(date)*, at *(Group Guide's home)*, beginning promptly at *(time)*.

Dreams in Motion will be the focus of our next session. In order to prepare for this session and maximize our time together, please write your vision for the end of one year. Remember to write your vision as if it has already happened. The notes that were taken during this session will be helpful in crafting your vision. Please bring a copy of your completed vision handout for each member of the group.

In addition to finishing your vision, there is another Session Accelerator that we'll all need to complete prior to our next session. We have just finished our fifth session, and this is a great time to do a survey to collect our feedback. It's called the Women Connected Tune-Up, and it will give us an opportunity to discuss what's working and what needs improving, and to offer suggestions to make our group the best that we can be. It will take approximately 30-45 minutes to complete the survey, and it will be worth every minute that you invest. *(Pass out Handout 5.4 and Session Accelerators 6.1 and 6.2)*

Please choose a new Growth Buddy and decide when you will be connecting for the first time.

Afterthoughts

Playing with possibilities, laughing, and talking about future dreams; this is how we connect. Women have done this since the dawn of time, connecting with one another through conversations that expand thinking and possibilities for an improved future. We have engaged in this process with our friends and our families, and today we do it for ourselves. How great is that? Did you notice the increased volume of the sound in the room as you participated in the sharing of your dreams?

If you dream big, really big, it creates energy and movement in your life. I encourage you to share your Future Perfect as often as possible. The more you share your dreams with others, the more you'll begin to believe that they are going to come true. So go ahead and embrace your dreams, your Future Perfect. It's fun, energizing, and a great way to live your life. Besides, there is no time like the present.

Our next session, Dreams in Motion, will assist you in bringing your dreams into reality.

Far away there in the sunshine are my highest aspirations. I may not reach them, but I can look up and see their beauty, believe in them, and try to follow where they lead.

☐ LOUISA MAY ALCOTT

Handout 5.1

FUTURE PERFECT NOTES

ROUND 1 It is *(one year from today's date)*. Your life is perfect in every way. Describe it in present tense language.

ROUND 2 Share the same perfect life. And add: What were the major obstacles or fears that you overcame during the past year? Remember, they have already been overcome!

ROUND 3 Share the same perfect life. And add: Who were the key people and resources that were involved in making your dreams come true?

ROUND 4 Share the same perfect life.
What are you personally most proud of having created?

Handout 5.2

CAPTURING WHAT MATTERS MOST TO ME

☐   What was most valuable to you in this session?

☐   What is it like to imagine a life that is perfect in every way?
    Were you able to act as if it was possible?

☐   How are you feeling in this moment?

Handout 5.3

MY COMMITMENTS

> I think the key is for women not to set
> any limits.

□ MARTINA NAVRATILOVA

Today's Date _____

Commitment _____

_____

_____

Date completed _____

Commitment _____

_____

_____

Date completed _____

Commitment _____

_____

_____

Date completed _____

Handout 5.4

SAMPLE VISION STATEMENTS

Selections from Vision Statements created in Women Connected groups

VISION SAMPLE 1

My office is an inviting and motivating space that has helped me become a successful salesperson. It is filled with inspiration that keeps me focused, involved, and balanced. My shelves are full of books, photos, organic materials, and art that reminds me of passions and endeavors beyond my desk. I am successful in my career. I have made many friends and business colleagues through networking events, and by being open to meeting and getting to know new people. I have established new, prosperous accounts through my knowledge of my marketplace and by being personable with my customers. I go the extra mile to make my business succeed—attention to detail is my calling card. My success in sales is affording me the financial means to explore and create other passions in my life.

VISION SAMPLE 2

Socially I have put myself out there and taken risks, and have let go of what the outcome might be. I have met a loving, caring man who loves to be with me. I feel comfortable and confident that I have met my life partner. I look forward to building a family. I am proud of the work I have done, coaching myself to love myself and all the amazing gifts I bring to this world.

VISION SAMPLE 3

Health: I have reached my weight goal by eating healthy foods and working out at least three times a week. I have so much more energy, and love feeling great. The energy I used to spend on wishing I was in shape is now used on other things in my life. My husband and I have been golfing a lot, and I'm actually getting better. We have been on several hikes this past summer, including Mount St. Helens. I've also begun to really relax by getting monthly massages.

VISION SAMPLE 4

I have really had fun this year with my creative side. My flowers and garden look beautiful and well kept. I do flower arranging when I want to. I have also painted some furniture, done several craft projects around the house, and learned card stamping. I love the new window treatments in my living room, which I found and put up. I also love the new ceiling painting I created in our dining room, and I had the lights in our home replaced.

Session Accelerator 6.1

WOMEN CONNECTED TUNE-UP

Please answer the following questions.

1. What has been the best thing for you about being in the group?

2. What has been most challenging thing for you about being in the group?

3. What has been the most nurturing and supportive thing about being in the group?

4. What in your life has been affected as a consequence of your participation in the group?

5. What conflicts, if any, do you see existing or possibly emerging in the near future in the group? How might we address these conflicts?

6. What changes can we implement to improve or enhance our effectiveness as a Women Connected group?

Your responses to these questions will be shared with the group during the next session. In order to have a successful group, open and honest dialogue is necessary on a regular basis.

Session Accelerator 6.2

MY VISION

Dreams
in Motion

I've been asked many times: "How did you succeed?"
The answer is I was middle-aged, had varicose veins,
and didn't have time to fool around.

☐ MARY KAY

My purpose in life is to make meaningful connections between people that can further their growth and happiness. It's the one thing I can't avoid doing; I *must* do it. I've learned that when I'm blocked from connecting people and connecting with others, I get stuck.

Several years ago I began getting requests from the women in my groups: "Why don't you write a book?" At first I didn't see a connection between what I love to do (connecting people) and writing a book. I thought it sounded like a good idea, a beautiful dream, but I didn't move forward with it. For eight years I talked about writing a book. Nothing happened. I thought a lot about it, I set up systems where I would need to be accountable, I felt that it was important, and there were people in my life encouraging me. But the bottom line was, I didn't do it. My dream got stuck and certainly wasn't in motion.

129

The shift into motion occurred when I realized that by putting Women Connected into a book, I could take what I was doing with small groups and make it available to women in all parts of the world, not just in my own backyard. Even after this realization, however, I needed goals to get into action. Once I actually committed to writing the book, I spent four months spinning my wheels before I realized that writing as a solitary activity wasn't going to work for me. It was agonizing; I just wasn't writing. It was only when I began asking my friends, relatives, and editor to sit down and talk with me about what I wanted to say—when I began to connect with other women face-to-face so that the book became about expressing my purpose—that the life experiences and information I wanted to share came pouring out of me. The book began to write itself!

When I am able to connect a goal with the experience I want to create in the world, and when that experience is aligned with my purpose, I am suddenly able to go over, around, under, or through whatever obstacles arise. This becomes possible because I'm absolutely clear that this motion, this essential action, is a direct expression of my dreams and my purpose in life.

This session is meant to catapult you into action. You've looked at your pur-

pose, and you've crafted a statement that expresses the way you want to bring your unique gifts into the world. Now it's time to create a compelling list of 20 Dreams in Motion you want to fulfill in your life this year. Every one of these dreams will be aligned with your purpose and vision. Making this list connects you to something bigger than yourself. Seeing your dreams as action points evokes the highest and best in you. It fuels your mind, body, and spirit with inspiration. Not only do you have the power and energy of your work and commitment moving you forward, you begin to discover that you are not alone! Women Connected is your support, your jump start, your cheering section, your sounding board. Your group is right here to help you take action.

With the help of your Women Connected coaching group, you will generate ideas outside the box, giving you a fresh, expansive vision of your future. Practicality and realism are great tools, but we get stuck when we habitually approach life as an endless to-do list of the routine and familiar. As Marian Wright Edelman says, "There comes a time when you roll up your sleeves and put yourself at the top of your commitment list." And there's no time like the present.

Words of Wisdom

KEEP THOUGHTS OF SUCCESS FOR YOUR-SELF AND THE GROUP AT THE FOREFRONT

Examine where you procrastinate and where you get stuck. Are you choosing dreams you think you *should* complete, or those that really speak to you?

DREAM BIG!

Be sure that the 20 Dreams in Motion list aligns with your vision and purpose. Be bold. There are some risks you can't afford not to take!

SHARE YOUR VISION

It's a great practice to share your vision whenever you get the opportunity. The more you talk about your vision, the more real it becomes (remember our activity in the Future Perfect session), and the likelihood of it happening is greatly increased.

Bumps in the Road—With Solutions!

LISTEN DEEPLY TO YOUR NEEDS AND THE NEEDS OF OTHERS

When we don't listen, we miss opportunities to hear profound ideas and feelings that enrich our connection to each other and expand our perspective.

Solution: Stop, take a deep breath, refocus, and consciously be present to your own and others' dreams, statements of purpose, and visions.

BE UNREASONABLE

Most of us think of ourselves as reasonable people. Unfortunately, reasonable people tend to get reasonable results! Now, before you think that this is just a trick of language, stop and really think about what this means. When we think of the future, often we think only in terms of familiar scenarios because they seem easily achievable, reasonable, and possible. To create an inspiring list of 20 Dreams in Motion, we must go beyond our usual *reasonable* way of looking at our lives.

Solution: Ask yourself whether your 20 Dreams list is a rehash of New Year's resolutions, goal lists, or other attempts you've made in the past to create a better life for yourself. If it is, it probably won't serve its intended purpose. Call on the group wisdom to help you connect to your heart's desire. When the list is *finished*, you can always do a reality check with your group members by asking, "Do you believe I can accomplish this in 12 months?"

RESISTANCE, EXCUSES, AND BROKEN COMMITMENTS

The energetic high of something new—Women Connected—may have begun to wear off. You might notice women feeling stuck and hear an increase of excuses for not following through with commitments.

This is a common process when change begins to take place. I like the way author Barbara Sher says it: "Everything you put in your way is just a method of putting off the hour when you could actually be doing your dream."

Solution: It takes perseverance and courage to change long-standing patterns. Be patient with yourself, and ask for support when you begin to hear yourself make excuses. Doing the difficult emotional and behavioral work that is required to change requires forward motion and lots of support. Aren't you the wise one for joining Women Connected?

Lori's Story

Lori is the mother of two little girls aged five and two, Mara and Ava. Formerly employed in a large corporate sales department, Lori had always known she was going to stay home to raise her children. She once told me, "When you stay at home, it's easy to focus all your time on your kids and forget your own dreams. Women Connected helped me stay focused and accountable." Lori has a smile that makes people smile back. Her friends unanimously describe her as extremely loyal and generous. Somehow, despite the demands of caring for her two young daughters and a household, Lori finds time to do volunteer work, raising money for programs serving at-risk youth.

When Lori created her 20 Dreams list, she thought about all the activities vying for her attention, and knew that without the support of her Women Connected group none of her dreams would come true. For years she had socked away several entrepreneurial ideas—most of them creative inventions—but as a busy mother with a thousand demands on her time, she had never ended up with a product in hand that she could sell.

Her big dream was to earn enough through her inventions (all child-focused products) to donate a significant portion of her profits to improve the lives of children in need. Lori drew on this sense of purpose and the enthusiastic support of her Women Connected group to design three products, for which she went on to register three patents. She faced many obstacles and setbacks, but she persevered. When I last spoke with her, Lori was diligently working to bring those products to market.

She didn't know it couldn't be done, so she went ahead and did it.

☐ MARY'S ALMANAC

The Big Picture: Dreams in Motion

Suggested Time Frames	Activity	Purpose	Materials | Set-up
:05	Opening	Welcome; transition into Women Connected; become present	• Poem
:20	Check-In	Update, reconnect, report	• Candle for each woman • Completed Session Accelerator 5.1 My Purpose
:30	Women Connected Tune-Up	Discuss what is working, what needs improvement, and how to initiate changes to make the group more powerful	• Completed Session Accelerator 6.1 Women Connected Tune-Up
1:15	Session: Dreams in Motion	Design small, creative, and compelling steps that will move dreams forward	• Completed Session Accelerator 6.2 My Vision • Handout 6.1 My 20 Dreams in Motion • Handout 6.2 Wisdom Blast
:05	Capturing What Matters Most to Me	Highlight session insights that are most relevant to your life	• Personal journal or Handout 6.3 Capturing What Matters Most to Me
:05	My Commitments	Increase accountability, intention, and likelihood of successful goal attainment	• Handout 6.4 My Commitments
:05	Closing Circle	Complete the session	• Standing circle • Extinguish candles
:05	Logistics for next session	Ensure Group continuity and clarity of requirements for the next session.	• Designate Group Guide, time, and place of next meeting • Choose a new Growth Buddy • Session Accelerator 7.1 My Underlying Beliefs

What You'll Need

- Poem
- Candle for each woman
- Digital timer
- Personal journal or notebook
- Calendar for setting next session's date
- Session Accelerator 5.1 My Purpose
- Session Accelerator 6.1 Women Connected Tune-Up
- Session Accelerator 6.2 My Vision
- Handout 6.1 My 20 Dreams in Motion
- Handout 6.2 Wisdom Blast
- Handout 6.3 Capturing What Matters Most to Me
- Handout 6.4 My Commitments
- Session Accelerator 7.1 My Underlying Beliefs

All handouts and Session Accelerators are provided as downloadable files at www.WomenConnected.com

What Happens During the "Dreams in Motion" Session

0:00 WELCOME (5 MINUTES)

Prior to starting the group, place a candle for each woman near the location where the group will be gathered. Each woman will light a candle at the completion of her Check-In.

Group Guide welcomes the group to her home and this session.

Let's begin by taking three or four deep breaths. As you inhale, breathe deeply into all the possibilities waiting to be discovered. As you exhale, sink deeply into your authentic self and relax into a state of openness and connection to self, and a realization that it's time to put your Dreams into Motion.

Group Guide reads her preselected poem.
After the poem is read say:
Silently affirm to yourself the intention you're holding for this session. How will you show up for today's session, what will you contribute, and how will you demonstrate your support to the group?

Allow one minute of quiet reflection and then proceed to Check-In.

0:05 CHECK-IN (20 MINUTES)

Let's begin our Check-In. Each person has two to three minutes to share her thoughts on the following topics:

☐ Take out Session Accelerator: My Purpose, and read your purpose to the group.

☐ Report the status of your last session's commitment.

☐ What has happened for you since our last session?

Who would like to begin?

Remember that the Group Guide will model the time frame for Check-In. Tell the group that you'll be using the digital timer, and that when the two minutes are up, the next person to her right checks in. Be sure to stay within the two-minute time frame.

As each individual completes her Check-In, she lights a candle and states her intention for the session.

After Check-In is completed, proceed to the next activity.

0:25 WOMEN CONNECTED TUNE-UP (30 MINUTES)

Instruct group to take out their completed Session Accelerator 6.1.

This session marks the sixth time we have come together as Women Connected. It's a good time to check in with one another and share our thoughts and feelings about how our group is functioning. As a result of the information shared in the Tune-Up, we might want to revisit our Connecting Principles (from Chapter 2) and make some changes or additions.

Here's how the process will go: We'll each share our response to Question 1, engage in a brief discussion, and then continue to

Question 2. This process will be repeated until we all have had the opportunity to share our thoughts related to each of the six questions.

The Group Guide's responsibility is to keep the conversation on track: making certain that each person speaks her mind and ensuring that the process moves along. It can be easy to get bogged down here if you're not intentional. When the group comes to Questions 5 and 6, assign a scribe to record the concerns and suggestions for change. The group will need to decide if changes need to be made to the Connecting Principles. It's important that each woman feels her point of view matters. Occasionally a group will have some bumps that need to be worked out, and it will take more time than is allotted for this activity. If this is the case with your group and there is a high level of interest in discussing the questions, ask the group if they want to lengthen today's session. If this is not possible, you can spend the entire session on the Tune-Up and postpone Dreams in Motion to your next session. Just remember, if you choose this option, it is still important to complete Capturing What Matters Most to Me, My Commitments, and Closing Circle before you end the session.

Remember that before the group discusses Questions 5 and 6, you'll need to assign someone to record the group's concerns and suggestions for change.

Who would like to volunteer to record our

responses to Question 5 and 6? Let's have a discussion on how we want to address these issues so that our group can continue to move forward in successful and powerful ways.

When the group has completed the Tune-Up, move on to the focus of this session: Dreams in Motion.

INTRODUCTION TO DREAMS IN MOTION

Today's session is Dreams in Motion. The purpose of this session is to bring your future vision into reality. During this session we will create a series of small steps that will move our dreams forward—creative and compelling steps that bring our future into reality.

0:55 SHARING OUR VISION (15 MINUTES)

Instruct group to take out completed Session Accelerator 6.2.

We now have the opportunity to share our individual visions with the entire group. It is important for us to listen deeply to the collective visions of our group. We are the support structure for turning one another's dreams into reality. Who would like to begin?

After the visions have been shared, the Group Guide says:

During the next 10 minutes we will be working alone and in silence.

Now that we've heard all of the remarkable visions that our group wants to create this year, it's time to design smaller steps to move our future dreams forward.

1:10 20 DREAMS IN MOTION (10 MINUTES)

Distribute Handout 6.1

Each one of us will create a list of the 20 Dreams we want to accomplish this year. Reflect on your Purpose Statement and your Vision. What would it take to bring these dreams forward into your life in powerful ways? Take a few minutes in silence to gather your thoughts. Then make your list. Focus your list on dreams that aren't dependent on someone else. For example, if you want to go to a spa with your sister, what happens if your sister isn't interested in going? It's better to simply write "A visit to the spa" as one of your 20 Dreams, so that it's not dependent on any particular person going with you, even though that might be nice! We'll have 10 minutes to work on this task. Let's stretch ourselves; write down all the dreams you'd like to set in motion this year. I will be the timekeeper.

Group Guide sets the digital timer.

At the end of 10 minutes, check in with the group and determine how many dreams each individual has listed. There are usually five to 15 dreams listed on each woman's handout.

Then you might say something like:
Now that you've got a head start on the Dreams in Motion list, it's time to do a Wisdom Blast to expand our lists by accessing the experiences and resources of the group.

1:20 WISDOM BLAST (50 MINUTES)

This activity lasts 50 minutes. Allow five minutes for the set-up and 45 minutes for the Wisdom Blast. Divide the number of women present into 45 minutes to determine the time for each woman. I suggest spending no more than five minutes per person. If there is extra time left, I encourage you to facilitate a brief discussion, focusing on the group's experience of the Wisdom Blast.

Distribute Handout 6.2

Please take a moment and read the description of a Wisdom Blast.

Wait a couple of minutes until everyone appears to have finished reading the handout.

Here are a few examples of questions that have been brought to a Wisdom Blast:

- ☐ I want to try something new every week. What can I do?
- ☐ How can I stop procrastinating?
- ☐ I need advice on how to determine what dreams are connected with my purpose.
- ☐ I'd like suggestions on how I can actually act on my vision.

The Wisdom Blast process will look like this:

- ☐ Each woman will begin by reading her vision to the group.
- ☐ Then she'll share her Dreams in Motion list.
- ☐ Lastly, she'll ask the group for advice in a specific area.

It's okay to ask a few questions for clarification, but the bulk of our time will be spent offering advice.

Who wants to go first?

Now it's time for the Wisdom Blast. We'll take *(number)* minutes for each person. The group will offer as many ideas as they can think of in the allotted time. These ideas need to be in alignment with the individual's vision.

- ☐ What can she do to make her vision a reality?
- ☐ What dreams need to be put into motion?

You'll not want to miss any of these great suggestions. Growth Buddies will write down the ideas for one another. I'll be the timekeeper and set the digital timer for *(number)* minutes. Let's begin.

The Group Guide's role is to keep the Wisdom Blast process moving. As soon as one woman is finished, ask Who's next? Then reset the digital timer.

At the completion of the Wisdom Blast you might say something like:
Wow—this group certainly knows how to give great advice!

Then proceed to the next activity.

2:10 CAPTURING WHAT MATTERS MOST TO ME (5 MINUTES)
Distribute Handout 6.3

We'll spend the next five minutes in silence and capture our thoughts and feelings about this session. Please take out your personal journal or use the handout to capture what matters most from today's session.

As you journal about this session, you might ask yourself:
☐   What was most valuable to me in this session?
☐   How did the Wisdom Blast assist me in this session?
☐   How am I feeling in this moment?

I'll be the timekeeper and set the digital timer for five minutes.

When time is up you might ask:
Would anyone like to share one of her comments with the group?

Take a minute or two to hear a few comments and then continue on to the next activity.

2:15 MY COMMITMENTS (5 MINUTES)
Distribute Handout 6.4
Take a moment to decide what you'd like to commit to between now and our next session. Think of a commitment that is aligned with your Dreams in Motion list. It can be a small step that moves you closer to where you want to be at the end of this year. After we write our commitments, we'll each take a turn sharing our commitments with the group.

After everyone has written her commitments, say:

We'll take a few minutes and share our commitments with each other. Start by stating your commitments and why they are important to you at this time in your life. Who would like to go first?

After the last woman has shared her commitments, thank the group and proceed to the Closing Circle.

2:20 CLOSING CIRCLE (5 MINUTES)

As we come to the end of this session, let's stand and form a circle. Take a moment to think of a word or brief thought that expresses what you experienced in the Dreams in Motion session.

Rotating around the Circle, each woman shares her word or thoughts. After everyone has shared in Closing Circle, say:

This session is complete. Please extinguish your candle until we connect again.

2:25 WHAT'S NEXT—MYTHOLOGY OF ME (5 MINUTES)

Ask for a volunteer to be the Group Guide for the next session. Remind the group that a different group member will take on the role of Group Guide during the next five sessions. Ask the group to take out their calendars to find an available date for the next session.

Our next session will be hosted by *(Group Guide's name)*, on *(date)*, at *(Group Guide's home)*, beginning promptly at *(time)*.

The topic of the next session is The Mythology of Me. In order to maximize our time together, please complete the Session Accelerator: Underlying Beliefs. *(Pass out Session Accelerator 7.1.)*

Choose a new Growth Buddy and decide when you will be connecting for the first time.

Afterthoughts

Change can be scary, exhilarating, and the best thing that ever happened to you! Sometimes in the process of writing down your dreams and sharing them with supportive friends, resistance can begin to rear its ugly head. You might notice yourself making excuses, putting things off, and not completing your commitments. The predictability of your current life can give you a false sense of security and comfort. Over time we get used to accepting less than we're capable of because it's so familiar.

Staying comfortable and refusing to grow, change, or challenge yourself, will eventually lead to a life of regrets. As difficult as it may be to change, remember this: you are not alone. Author Iyanla Vanzant gives us encouragement with these words of wisdom: "Challenges come so we can grow and be prepared for things we are not equipped to handle now. When we face our challenges with faith, prepared to learn, willing to make changes, and if necessary, to let go, we are demanding our power to be turned on." When you recognize that resistance is showing up, yell for help, call your Growth Buddy, do something to stay in motion. A world of new possibilities awaits you, and now is the time to work through the resistance and move into your dreams. As you move through the bumps in the road, keep in mind the words of Pulitzer Prize winning poet Mary Oliver:

"Tell me, what is it you plan to do with your one wild and precious life?"

☐ MARY OLIVER

Handout 6.1
MY 20 DREAMS IN MOTION

1.	11.
2.	12.
3.	13.
4.	14.
5.	15.
6.	16.
7.	17.
8.	18.
9.	19.
10.	20.

Handout 6.2
WISDOM BLAST

This is a process designed to access the group's collective wisdom. It is a brainstorming session, and any idea is worth listening to. Sometimes the best ideas come out of left field! Each woman has the option to bring an issue, challenge, or dilemma before the group. For three minutes, the group generates as many ideas as possible to help address the issue. This is the only time when giving advice is encouraged.

The role of the group is to stay focused, with the intention of providing solutions to the problem described. The role of the recipient is to listen, without comment or judgments. Just stay present, focused, and open to receiving the wisdom from the group.

The recipient's Growth Buddy will capture all ideas generated by the group. Before the next session, look over this list and choose what you believe to be the best solution. Try out the solution and report back to the group during the next Check-In.

Handout 6.3

CAPTURING WHAT MATTERS MOST TO ME

☐   What was most valuable to me in this session?

☐   How did the Wisdom Blast assist me in this session?

☐   How am I feeling in this moment?

The future belongs to those who believe in the
beauty of their dreams.

☐ ELEANOR ROOSEVELT

Today's Date _____

Commitment _____

_____

_____

Date completed _____

Commitment _____

_____

_____

Date completed _____

Commitment _____

_____

_____

Date completed _____

Session Accelerator 7.1
MY UNDERLYING BELIEFS

Underlying beliefs, if left unexamined, have the ability to influence our choices and keep us stuck in the past. In order to be our best selves and move our dreams into reality, we need to bring our beliefs into the open and examine them as if they were brand new.

This Session Accelerator will take about 30 minutes. As you write your response to each statement, be quick and write the first thought that comes to mind. Don't censor yourself or second-guess your thoughts. Whatever you write is absolutely perfect. You will be sharing this Session Accelerator with a partner during The Mythology of Me session.

Write your first response to the following:

When it comes to

Decision-making, I

Being visionary, or being able to create the future, I

Challenging others' thinking, I

Listening, I

Being rigorous, I

Being able to objectively see multiple perspectives at once, I

Using my intuition, I

Prioritizing and keeping things on track, I

When it comes to

Communicating, I

Resolving conflicts, I

Building trust and loyalty, I

Being in conflict, I

Keeping my word, I

People having messy personal lives, I

Control, I

Acknowledging or recognizing others, I

Being acknowledged, I

Change, I

Working in partnership, I

Something I'm afraid to say or do, I

Making mistakes, I

Being courageous when talking about things that
are difficult to talk about, I

When it comes to

Being challenged by others, I

Others correcting me, I

Getting my needs met, I

Being intimate, I

Holding others accountable, I

Being a bearer of bad news, I

Expressing myself fully, I

Being authentic, I

Being angry, I

Being sad, I

Being lonely, I

Being supported by others, I

Forgiving and letting go, I

Playing and being joyful, I

The Mythology of Me

> We are all on a spiral path.
> No growth takes place in a straight line. There will be
> setbacks along the way . . . There will be shadows, but they
> will be balanced by patches of light . . .
> Awareness of the pattern is all you need to sustain you
> along the way.
>
> ☐ KRISTEN ZAMBUCKA

A myth, according to my dad's old *Webster's Dictionary*, is "a story, the origin of which is forgotten" or "a person or thing existing only in imagination." We all carry within us stories about ourselves; some of them are true and others are false. When you don't know who you are, it's easy to be fooled into believing just about anything. When you're not sure what your truth is, there's a tendency to live as if the myths—the false stories you carry inside—are true.

I want to tell you about woman I know named Joy. After being married and divorced twice, she had given up on men. Joy concluded she was too picky, that she expected too much from a relationship, and she felt there weren't any men available with whom she'd be happy for the long haul. She told anyone who would listen, "I always end up unhappy in romantic relationships; therefore, I just shouldn't be in one."

After avoiding going out with a number of interested men, she found herself communicating long-distance with a friend at work. Like Joy, this man traveled frequently doing corporate training and didn't have a lot of time for dating. After three months of increasingly satisfying long-distance conversations, the two decided to meet. "It was awkward," she said, "I thought he looked like a Boy Scout, not my type at all." But she went home from that first date and reported this to one of her best friends, Carol, who said, "You've finally met someone who sounds like he's healthy!"

It was the first time Joy had ever considered that perhaps it had been her past choices, not her personal aptitude for relationships, that had caused her marriages to end in divorce. The myth Joy had been telling herself—There aren't any men available that I'd be happy with for the long haul—had proven to be false. As of this writing, Joy and Allen will soon celebrate

149

their fourteenth year of happy married life. That old myth is history! As long as we remain captive to the limiting mythologies of our lives, we aren't free to create the kind of life we dream about.

This session of Women Connected dramatically increases your awareness of how you think about yourself. This is important because the stories you believe about yourself literally shape the life you live—these are the stories that support your vision and purpose, and they're also the ones that undermine you. For example, maybe you're someone who's good at looking on the bright side of things, and this skill sustains you in hard times. On the other hand, you may have used that same ability to create a myth— I'll always be provided for—but you haven't done your part to make this true. Your self-talk may be false *(I don't have to worry about charging all these purchases on my credit card because I'll be provided for)*, yet it influences your behavior and you act as if your myths are true. The more you repeat a myth, the stronger it becomes. Eventually you convince yourself and others that it's a solid fact. Often the result is not what you had envisioned at all.

It's time to stop believing myths about yourself—time to take inventory and look squarely at the truth. In this session, it's good to really level with yourself about who you are today. Tell yourself about the wonderful gifts you bring to the world. Notice the places in your life that you're not so happy about, too. Once you begin to do this, it will quickly become obvious that the more you focus on your best qualities, the more easily you begin to realize your dreams. As you get better and better at encouraging yourself in this way, you'll watch the obstacles to your success disappear before your eyes.

As you tell your Women Connected group about the limiting stories you've believed about yourself, it's easier to see how foolish many of them are. Speaking private thoughts out loud, exposing your personal myths to the sunlight of the group's awareness, suddenly frees you from repeating them over and over to yourself. You can choose to delete those stories, or you can edit them and retell them in ways that empower you.

This session is a special time to listen deeply to one another and experience meaningful connection. Everyone has at least one false story; some of us have more. We can support each other in creating stories that reflect who we are today: women who are bringing their best selves forward and living into their dreams. One of my heroes, Oprah Winfrey, tells us, "It isn't until you come to a spiritual understanding of who you are—not necessarily a religious feeling, but deep down, the spirit within—that you can begin to take control." And I say, there's no time like the present!

Words of Wisdom

LISTEN FOR THEMES THAT CONTRIBUTE TO THE MYTHS IN YOUR LIFE

If you tend to tell yourself things like "It's okay to settle for less in some situations" or "I don't need very much to be satisfied," consider how those limiting thoughts might be tied to a particular myth, such as "I am not worthy of a wonderful life."

BE WILLING TO QUESTION YOUR ASSUMPTIONS, AND INVITE OTHERS TO QUESTION THEM

Over time, our myths begin to live as the truth in our minds. Without feedback from others, it's almost impossible to see the myths about ourselves. With an open mind and a listening ear, you'll get much more out of this session.

The beginning of wisdom is calling things by their right names.

☐ CHINESE PROVERB

BE GENTLE AND COMPASSIONATE WITH YOURSELF

Every one of us lives with a few false ideas about herself. Remember, whenever you tell yourself "This is the way I am," you may be cutting off valuable information that could improve your life, and you may be limiting your capacity to love and be loved. Be kind to yourself, while staying curious about yourself and your long-held beliefs.

Bumps in the Road—With Solutions!

MAKING YOURSELF WRONG

You get caught up in blaming yourself or beating yourself up for decisions made in the past.

Solution: Acknowledge you were doing the best you could do at the time.

THE SELF-CRITIC IS DIFFICULT TO SILENCE

You get stuck in negative opinions of yourself and feel like it's a downward spiral.

Solution: Give yourself three minutes (maximum!)—set a timer—to think about (and wallow in) what a terrible person you are, then write everything down on a piece of paper, crush it up, and either burn it or throw it in the trash where it belongs.

Gretchen's Story

My very first impression of Gretchen was that she hardly took up any space. In fact, she seemed to disappear in her Women Connected group. She had short dark hair, a reluctant smile, and I noticed she said

"I'm sorry" a lot. A single mother with three children, she had been physically abused by both her ex-husbands. After her five-year-old witnessed her being attacked by the child's father, she left the marriage and stopped trusting her choices in men. Gretchen's oldest child, a son, had just been placed in a care center for drug-addicted teenagers. Gretchen's main guideline in life had become, "I'll never again bring another abusive man into my life or my children's lives."

When I first met Gretchen, she had just landed a job in a small bank, doing work that frequently took her out into the community. Gretchen was a bright, loyal worker, and her boss really believed in her abilities. I watched with delight as she began to get positive feedback about the great work she was doing. With support from her Women Connected group, Gretchen began to hold her head a bit higher. Being in Women Connected was her first experience of long-term friendships with other women.

The group challenged a central myth Gretchen believed about herself: that she was a poor chooser of men and for this reason should never marry again. She had collected a lifetime of evidence that she used again and again to support her myth that men would always be unkind to her. She also spent a good portion of her adult life half-believing she deserved whatever

she got. But as she heard from her Women Connected group that they saw her as loving and deserving of love, and as they shared about the caring men they had known, little by little Gretchen gathered courage and self-esteem. As the members of her group encouraged her, she began to examine the validity of her evidence and started to look for ways to create a different and better story to live into. As a beginning step, she joined a church where she felt she might meet someone more in alignment with the new story she was creating about who she was and what she deserved.

About two years after Gretchen's Women Connected coaching group stopped meeting, I ran into her in town. She looked like an entirely different woman. She was radiant! Her son, who had received care for drug addiction, was now doing extremely well. As a result of her son's difficulty, Gretchen had become involved in helping and supporting other parents of addicted teenagers. Discovering how much she had to give to others had truly transformed Gretchen's life. She also proudly shared with me that she was now happily married to a man who loved her and treated her well. Gretchen had found the strength and support to live into a new and different story. She had traded a myth about herself for a truth that reflected who she really was.

The Big Picture: The Mythology of Me

Suggested Time Frames	Activity	Purpose	Materials | Set-up
:05	Opening	Welcome; transition into Women Connected; become present	• Poem
:20	Check-In	Update, reconnect, report	• Candle for each woman
:30	Dreams in Motion	Fine-tune Dreams in Motion and check for alignment with Purpose and Vision	• Completed Handout 6.1 My 20 Dreams in Motion
1:15	Session: The Mythology of Me	Discover stories about oneself that are unproductive and false. Gather evidence to demonstrate that these myths are no longer true.	• Completed Session Accelerator 7.1 My Underlying Beliefs • Personal journal or notebook
:05	Capturing What Matters Most to Me	Highlight session insights that are most relevant to your life	• Personal journal or Handout 7.1 Capturing What Matters Most to Me
:05	My Commitments	Increase accountability, intention, and likelihood of successful goal attainment	• Handout 7.2 My Commitments
:05	Closing Circle	Complete the session	• Standing circle • Extinguish candles
:05	Logistics for next session	Ensure Group continuity and clarity of requirements for the next session.	• Designate Group Guide, time, and place of next meeting • Choose a new Growth Buddy • Session Accelerator 8.1 What's the Evidence? • Session Accelerator 8.2 Collage of Possibilities

What You'll Need

- Poem
- Candle for each woman
- Digital timer
- Personal journal or notebook
- Extra paper for session notes
- Calendar for setting next session's date
- Handout 6.1 My 20 Dreams in Motion
- Session Accelerator 7.1 My Underlying Beliefs
- Handout 7.1 Capturing What Matters Most to Me
- Handout 7.2 My Commitments
- Session Accelerator 8.1 What's the Evidence?
- Session Accelerator 8.2 Collage of Possibilities

Session Accelerators and handouts are provided as downloadable files at www.WomenConnected.com

What Happens During "The Mythology of Me" Session

0:0 WELCOME (5 MINUTES)

Prior to starting the group, place a candle for each woman near the location where the group will be gathered. Each woman will light a candle at the completion of her Check-In.

Group Guide welcomes the women to her home and this session.

We'll begin this session by taking three or four deep breaths. As you inhale, breathe deeply into all the possibilities waiting to be discovered. As you exhale, sink deeply into your authentic self and relax into a state of openness and connection to self, and release any thoughts that drain your energy.

Group Guide reads her preselected poem.

After the poem is read say:

Silently affirm to yourself the intention you're holding for this session. How will you show up for today's session, what will you contribute, and how will you demonstrate your support to the group?

Allow one minute of quiet reflection and then proceed to Check-In.

0:05 CHECK-IN (20 MINUTES)

Let's begin our Check-In. Each person has two to three minutes to share her thoughts on the following topics:

- ☐ Status of your commitments
- ☐ Your Growth Buddy connection: how was it, what worked, and any suggested tune-ups?
- ☐ What I learned about myself since last session was . . .

Who would like to begin?

Remember that the Group Guide will model the time

frame for Check-In. Tell the group that you'll be using the digital timer, and that when the two minutes are up, the next person to her right checks in. Be sure to stay within the two-minute time frame.

As each individual completes her Check-In, she lights a candle and states her intention for the session.

After Check-In is completed, proceed to the next activity.

0:25 MY 20 DREAMS IN MOTION (20 MINUTES)

Instruct group to take out their completed Handout 6.1.

In order to ensure that the Dreams in Motion list is aligned with your purpose and vision, you'll spend time with your Growth Buddy going over your individual list of 20 Dreams. As you go through your Dream list, take a look at each dream. Is it realistic? Is it somewhat of a stretch? Is the dream dependent on anyone else but you? Ask yourself, "For the sake of what am I doing this?" Your answer to this question should be in alignment with either your purpose or your vision. It's important to be rigorous with your Dream list; you will be making weekly and monthly commitments to move them from dreams into reality. You'll have 10 minutes per person to fine-

tune your Dreams in Motion. I'll be the timekeeper and let you know when half the time has passed.

Are there any questions? *(pause)* Please begin.

Group Guide sets the digital timer for 10 minutes. When the time is up, say to group:
It is time to switch speakers. You have 10 minutes left for this activity.

Group Guides resets the digital timer for 10 minutes. When the time has passed, proceed to the Wrap Up of this activity.

0:45 DREAMS IN MOTION
LARGE GROUP DISCUSSION (10 MINUTES)

We'll take a few minutes now and discuss together the following questions:

- ☐ In what ways was it helpful to go over your Dream list with your Growth Buddy?
- ☐ What did you learn or experience as a result of this activity?

After approximately 10 minutes or less of discussion, you might say something like the following, as a transition to the next activity:

From the sound of it, there are some wonderful dreams that are being put into motion. However, sometimes our dreams don't come true because we hold limiting beliefs about ourselves. We hold on to old stories, old behavior patterns, and they can get in the way of our growth and keep us stuck. In today's session we'll be looking at ways to move beyond what may have limited us in the past.

0:55 INTRODUCTION TO THE MYTHOLOGY OF ME (5 MINUTES)

This session is The Mythology of Me. Most of us have a tendency to believe all kinds of stories about ourselves that aren't true. In fact, they're just myths. The scary thing about these myths is that they begin to take on a life of their own, so that in time we come to believe that they describe how we really are. We then live our lives as if those myths are entirely true. Today's session shines a light on the myths we've created about ourselves, myths that undermine our power and success. As Women Connected, we will identify these life-draining myths and replace them with stories about ourselves that reflect and support who we really are today!

1:00 MY UNDERLYING BELIEFS (30 MINUTES)

Ask the group to take out their completed Session Accelerator 7.1 and choose a partner for this activity.

Take a moment and decide which partner would like to go first in sharing your Underlying Beliefs statements. *(pause)* After you have read your list of statements and responses to your partner, respond to the following questions:

☐ What did you notice as you were writing responses to the incomplete phrases?

☐ What became clear to you?

☐ What seems to be the Myth of Your Life?

☐ How would you describe your feelings right now?

You'll have 15 minutes per person to share your thoughts and insights. I will be the timekeeper, and I'll let you know when half the time has passed.

Group Guide sets digital timer for 15 minutes.

After 15 minutes, tell the group that it's time for the second person to take her turn. Group Guide resets the digital timer for 15 minutes. When the 15 minutes has passed, proceed to the next activity.

1:30 JOURNAL WRITING (15 MINUTES)

Now we are going to take the information we've unearthed and use it in a process called automatic journal writing. We'll spend five minutes on this activity. It's quite simple; you'll write in your journal or notebook without lifting your pen until I say *Stop*. The purpose of this activity is to write down uncensored thoughts. If you spend time thinking, it will interrupt the flow of thoughts and your inner critic may get in the way. During this activity you will not pick up your pen from the paper at any time. Just continue writing on the topic for the entire five minutes. If you get stuck, write something you've written before, or just write *blah, blah, blah* until your mind frees up enough to write some more. You'll begin the journal topic with *I Am*, then you'll fill in the blank. List as many of your qualities as possible. Write thoughts about yourself that are great, good, and not so good, including those you dislike the most. I'll set the timer for five minutes. Are there any questions?

Okay, let's begin. *I am* . . .

Group Guide sets digital timer for five minutes.

After five minutes Group Guide says:
Take a moment and review what you've written. Then, from what you've written, choose two statements or beliefs about yourself that are *not* in alignment with the person you are becoming—the person who is committed to creating her Vision and living her Purpose this year. Place a mark next to these two beliefs.

Give the group a couple minutes to complete this.

Now choose two statements or beliefs that are in absolute agreement with the future you are creating from today going forward.

Again, give the group time to complete this. After a few minutes check in with the group, and when everyone is done, proceed to the next activity.

1:45 MY BELIEFS AND SUPPORTING EVIDENCE (5 MINUTES)

Instruct the group to take out two clean sheets of paper. Pause a moment, then say:

On a clean sheet of paper, list one positive belief at the top of the page. At the top of a second sheet of paper, list one negative belief. With each belief, do the following:

☐ List four or five pieces of evidence that proves this belief is true.

☐ List four or five pieces of evidence that proves this belief is false.

Tell the group that they have up to five minutes to complete this portion of the activity.

PARTNER ACTIVITY (10 MINUTES)

Choose a partner who will be your new Growth Buddy—if possible, someone you haven't worked with before.

Wait until everyone gets settled, then say:

Taking turns with your Growth Buddy, share both the positive and the negative beliefs that you wrote in your journal. Be sure to include the evidence that supports the belief being true, and the evidence that supports the belief being false. There is no need to process or discuss the beliefs; your job is to listen and focus all of your attention on the person who is speaking. I will be the timekeeper and let you know when to change speakers.

Group Guide sets digital timer for five minutes. When five minutes are up, ask the group to change speakers. Reset the digital timer for the remaining five minutes.

2:00 MY BELIEFS
LARGE GROUP DISCUSSION (10 MINUTES)

Facilitate a discussion using the following questions:

☐ What did you experience during the automatic journal writing?

☐ What was it like to share with your Growth Buddy the positive beliefs about yourself?

☐ How about the negative beliefs?

After about 10 minutes, proceed to the next activity.

2:10 CAPTURING WHAT MATTERS MOST TO ME (5 MINUTES)
Distribute Handout 7.1

We'll spend the next five minutes in silence to capture our thoughts and feelings about today's session. Please take out your personal journal or use the handout to capture what matters most from today's session.

As you journal about this session, you might ask yourself:
- ☐ What was most valuable to me in this session?
- ☐ What do I want to remember?
- ☐ What are the implications of being able to describe a belief from either point of view (true or not true)?

I'll be the timekeeper and set the digital timer for five minutes.

When time is up you might ask:
Would anyone like to share one of her comments with the group?

Take a minute or two and listen to a few comments, and then begin the next activity.

2:15 MY COMMITMENTS (5 MINUTES)

Distribute Handout 7.2

Take a moment to decide what you'd like to commit to do before our next session. It might be useful to think of a commitment that is aligned with creating your Future Perfect. Revisit your 20 Dreams in Motion list. The commitment you choose can be one small step that moves you closer to where you want to be at the end of this year. After we write our commitments, we'll each take a turn sharing our commitments with the group.

After everyone has written her commitments, say:
We'll take a few minutes and share our commitments with each other. Start by stating your commitment and why it is important to you at this time in your life. Who would like to go first?

After the last woman has shared her commitments, thank the group and proceed to the Closing Circle.

2:20 CLOSING CIRCLE (5 MINUTES)

As we come to the end of this session, let's stand and form a circle. Take a moment to think of a word or a brief thought that expresses what you experienced today in the Mythology of Me session.

Rotating around the Circle, each woman shares her word or thoughts. After everyone has shared in Closing Circle, say:
This session is complete. Please extinguish your candle until we connect again.

2:25 WHAT'S NEXT—THE BRAND OF ME (5 MINUTES)

Ask for a volunteer to be the Group Guide for the next session. Remind the group that each group member will take on the role of Group Guide at least once; by now some women will be volunteering for their second time. Ask everyone to take out her calendar to find an available date for the next session.

The next session will be hosted by *(Group Guide)*, on *(date)*, at *(Group Guide's home)*, beginning promptly at *(time)*.

Our next topic is The Brand of Me. In order to maximize our time together, there will be two Session Accelerators. The first one is What's the Evidence? Affirming or Rejecting Beliefs. This will take approximately 30 minutes to complete. The second Session Accelerator is the Collage of Possibilities, which will take approximately 30-45 minutes to complete. *(Pass out Session Accelerators 8.1 and 8.2.)*

Get together with the Growth Buddy you chose earlier in the session and decide when you'll be connecting for the first time.

Afterthoughts

All of us create stories and myths about ourselves. These stories and myths often reflect to us our level of personal development and self-awareness. Sometimes we create internal barriers, believe we are victims, or believe we are powerless. Sometimes other people or situations get in our way. If we are aware that our inner critic can be turned around to become our cheerleader and champion, then and only then can we make a different choice, take a different direction, and create more empowering stories. If we can describe these beliefs about ourselves from either a positive or negative point of view, it becomes clear that we are the ones choosing what we believe—and therefore we can just as readily make a different choice. This is a particularly powerful position to adopt when looking at beliefs that are no longer working in our lives.

We are each unique—made up of different likes, dislikes, and approaches to our world. And yet, we all share something in common: the desire to be happy, successful, and fulfilled, living a life full of loving and being loved. What would it be like for you to create stories that are life-affirming, filled with love, confidence, and inspiration? Now is the time for you to decide what new stories you'll create for yourself. As one of my favorite authors, Marianne Williamson, says, "We are always evolving toward either a smaller and more fearful self, or a larger and more loving self." Which one will it be? You choose.

Handout 7.1

CAPTURING WHAT MATTERS MOST TO ME

☐   What was most valuable to me in this session?

☐   What do I want to remember?

☐   What are the implications of being able to describe a belief from either point of view (true or not true)?

Handout 7.2

MY COMMITMENTS

> Your beliefs are never neutral.
> They either move you forward or hold you back.
> And you choose what you will believe.
>
> ☐ MARCIA WIEDER

Today's Date _____

Commitment _____

_____

_____

Date completed _____

Commitment _____

_____

_____

Date completed _____

Commitment _____

_____

_____

Date completed _____

Session Accelerator 8.1

WHAT'S THE EVIDENCE? AFFIRMING OR REJECTING BELIEFS

When you're stuck in a spiral, to change all aspects
of the spin you need only to change one thing.

☐ CHRISTINA BALDWIN

Choose one positive belief. Choose one negative belief. Between now and
our next session, gather evidence to support that the positive belief is true,
and evidence to support that the negative belief is false.

A POSITIVE BELIEF I HAVE ABOUT MYSELF IS:

The evidence that I have gathered that this positive belief is absolutely
TRUE:

A NEGATIVE BELIEF I HAVE ABOUT MYSELF IS:

The evidence that I have gathered that this negative belief is absolutely
FALSE:

Session Accelerator 8.2

COLLAGE OF POSSIBILITIES

Find a picture of yourself as a baby or toddler. If this is not possible, you can choose a favorite photo from your youth. Tape or glue your photo in the middle of a large sheet of paper (11x14 inches or larger). Spend 5-10 minutes looking at the photo. Ask yourself:

☐ What do I see in the eyes of this child?
☐ What is possible for this child?
☐ What are her dreams for the future?

Think about all aspects of her life—spiritual, emotional, financial, relationships, health, and anything else that occurs to you. Write your thoughts on the sheet surrounding the photo. We'll be sharing our Collages of Possibilities at our next session.

In addition to this photo, please bring your *most recent* favorite photo of yourself.

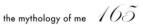

The

Brand

of Me

For the more you know yourself
the more you are able to impact others' lives.
There is a vitality, a life force, an energy, a quickening,
which is translated through you into action.
And because there is only one you this expression is unique,
and if you block it, it will never exist through any medium,
and the world will never have it.

□ MARTHA GRAHAM

What is The Brand of Me? Well, the dictionary says that to brand something means to "make an indelible mark or impression," and that a brand is "a distinctive type or kind." It's a popular activity these days for companies to discuss their branding strategies. Huge sums of money are expended in finding just the right branding strategy to take a product or company into the marketplace. The goal is for the customer to identify with the brand so completely that she will buy whatever product the company offers for sale.

Now, you might be asking yourself, "What does this have to do with me?" Wherever you go and whatever you do, your brand speaks loudly to everyone you come in contact with during the day. You make a distinctive impression that is your brand—the unique expression of your essential self. If it speaks of outdated beliefs or perceptions about yourself, then clearly

167

it's not an accurate branding strategy for you!

So what's your brand? What do you want to be known for? How do you take yourself out into the marketplace? Do people want to buy what you sell? And more important, is what they see what they really get? Is there a difference between how you perceive yourself and how others perceive you? Angeles Arrien, in her book *The Four-Fold Way*, shares with us, "When we are able to value our self-worth as much as we listen to the self-critic, we begin to tap the resource of wisdom." There is no time like the present to challenge your outdated beliefs and free yourself from the way you have been perceived in the past. Keep what works for you, and embrace what you want to live into—beginning today. It's your choice!

By this time in the Women Connected program, you've received feedback from group members. Does the feedback feel aligned with how you see yourself? Often we're surprised to find others see us as being able to achieve more than we think we can, and sometimes we discover that others have a higher opinion of us than we do of ourselves. This session is an opportunity to bring all of your creative energy into form through words, graphics, photos, and anything else that catches your imagination. View your life as your brand and decide how you want it to express it. During this session you'll create a unique and wonderful collage that represents the life you choose: The Brand of Me!

One of my favorite places to visit is Whidbey Island north of Seattle, where I love walking the beaches. Over the years I've discovered a special beach which is usually deserted; it's the kind of place where you can walk for miles without seeing a soul. To me, this beach has the perfect mixture of sand and stones. And since I've been collecting special stones since I was a little girl, I often feel like I've discovered heaven on earth. Recently while walking on the beach, it occurred to me that in many ways stones are like people. They come in all shapes and sizes, they have different colors and various weights, some of them I'm drawn to and others I seem to ignore. Just as in life, there are people who catch our eye and we want to be with, while others we walk by and barely notice.

Some brands catch our eye and others don't.

Every now and then I find an agate, which is a very special kind of stone. When held up to the light, it has an amber glow and I can see right though it. Nothing blocks its beauty, even though dark streaks might permeate it. Like the agate, every brand has its own beauty, its own transparency. Remember your Purpose, your Vision, and what makes your heart sing. You have the power to create who and what you want to be— The Brand of Me.

Words of Wisdom

THINK ABOUT WOMEN WHOM YOU ADMIRE

Before creating your Brand of Me collage, think about the women in your life whom you admire, who have been your role models. These women exemplify important aspects of your brand, since they reflect what you value and aspire to. Who are they and what makes them special? What are the unique qualities they possess that you'd like to incorporate into your life? Such a woman might be a close friend, a favorite relative, someone from the past, or a character in a book.

A dear friend of mine, Marley Rynd Cohen, was a powerful role model in my life. She died recently after living with a rare form of cancer for over five years. Marley's courage (although she didn't think she was the least bit courageous), her guts, her determination to live life on her own terms, her creative approach in whatever she did, and the devotion she had to her three sons and husband were a constant inspiration to me. Her can-do attitude reminded me that even in the darkest hours, there can be a glimmer of hope; that a beacon of light is visible at the end of the tunnel. I will carry her memory in my heart always. Marley has left a remarkable legacy that will continue to influence the lives of those who knew and loved her. What are you doing now that will keep on giving beyond your life?

IF YOU'RE WORRIED THAT YOU'RE NOT AN ARTIST, DON'T BE CONCERNED

Over the decades I've seen the most amazing collages, each unique; and very few of them have been created by professional artists. Every collage is an artistic creation, and you are the artist who will be creating this collage representing how you want to be seen as you go forward in your life. Whatever you make is a reflection of you.

The most visible creators I know of are those artists whose medium is life itself. The ones who express the inexpressible—without brush, hammer, clay, or guitar. They neither paint nor sculpt—their medium is being. Whatever their presence touches has increased life. They see and don't have to draw. They are the artists of being alive.

☐ AUTHOR UNKNOWN

BRING A LARGE NUMBER OF MAGAZINES TO THE SESSION

Ask your friends and neighbors for their old magazines. The more diversity in subject matter, the more choices you'll have for the collage. One of my neighbors, an engineer, gave me his old civil engineering magazines, and I found a remarkable bridge photograph that I used in my collage. I even asked my dentist for his used magazines. You never know what magazine will have the perfect word, picture, or colored background for your collage.

Bumps in the Road—With Solutions!

RUNNING OUT OF TIME

It is almost guaranteed that this activity will take more time than you've allotted for the session.

Solution: This creative activity is so much fun that you might want to consider lengthening the session. Much like the old quilting bees, when women and creativity come together, magical things can happen.

HAVING TROUBLE FINDING THE RIGHT WORD, PICTURE, OR IDEA

There is a good possibility that you might have difficulty finding the perfect picture that illustrates The Brand of You.

Solution: It's simple—just ask for help. You'll discover that your Women Connected friends will be more than happy to help you out. And they'll most likely need your help, as well.

SOMEONE IN THE GROUP THINKS THE ACTIVITY IS SILLY

There are women who haven't done any artwork since they were little girls. The last time they did any cut and paste activity they were in kindergarten. So it's is easy to understand why they might resist a collage activity.

Solution: Encourage participation. The end result of the activity is worth it. Each woman will use the collage to illustrate her story; to share how she wants to be seen and what her brand is. Believe me, it is worth being silly sometimes! At the end of this session you'll be glad that everyone participated.

Linda's Story

Linda is a rare mixture of seemingly competing opposites. Finnish roots show strongly in her modest and humble demeanor, and she also possesses the ability to switch gears, to be the center of attention and take charge in a very public way. A former flute player in a rock band, she is a world traveler, a scuba diver, and a loving wife, mother, and stepmother. In her chosen field of law, she is a trusted and respected leader, challenging her people and making certain they have the training and resources needed to excel in their professions. She never appears rattled, and when chaos and uncertainty show up, she exudes a calming presence, creating a feeling of security. As a friend, she is loyal and nonjudgmental, and can be counted on to keep your secrets.

Linda entered law to help people. And it was the *real* reason. In her private law firm, the first few years fed her core desire to help people. She was working with great clients who benefited from her experience and legal expertise. Then there was a change in leadership at her law firm, and the bottom line became more important than making people's lives better. The more they moved to bottom line management in the practice, the more out of integrity Linda felt. It was a slow process, taking place over many years. During the last three or four years of her employment with the firm, any time there was increased stress, Linda got an involuntary twitch in her left eye and a pain in her gut. Her body was giving her confirmation that something wasn't right in her world. Linda began to feel discouraged and couldn't imagine herself continuing in the legal profession. She felt lost and didn't know where to turn.

Linda had been a member of a Women Connected group for three years. She occasionally shared work-related concerns with her group, but this was dif-ficult; Linda had a history of self-reliance and didn't like asking for help. Through the years, women in Linda's group provided her with feedback, affirmed her concerns about the law firm, and were patient when Linda was confused. Mostly, the women just listened, reminded her of who she really was, and confirmed the unique gifts that she possessed. With this support, Linda became clearer about her brand, who she really wanted to be, and how she wanted to be seen and treated.

Eventually, Linda was asked to join the State Attorney General's office. The new position was a perfect fit for Linda, and her stress-related physical symptoms disappeared.

As Nobel Prize winning novelist Toni Morrison wrote: "Bit by bit . . . she had claimed herself. Freeing yourself was one thing; claiming ownership of that freed self was another."

Today, Linda is reaping the rewards and discovering the joys of "claiming ownership of that freed self." She is recognizing and deeply connecting with the unique brand that makes her who she is.

The Big Picture: The Brand of Me

Suggested Time Frames	Activity	Purpose	Materials | Set-up
:05	Opening	Welcome; transition into Women Connected; become present	• Poem
:20	Check-In	Update, reconnect, report	• Candle for each woman • My Purpose statement
:15	What's the Evidence?	Share discoveries related to the Myths of Me and the supporting evidence	• Completed Session Accelerator 8.1 What's the Evidence?
1:30	Session: The Brand of Me	Reconnect with the best parts of oneself and create a powerful visual reminder of what matters most	• Completed Session Accelerator 8.2 Collage of Possibilities • Poster paper, markers, colored pens, pencils • Magazines, scissors, glue
:05	Capturing What Matters Most to Me	Highlight session insights that are most relevant to your life	• Personal journal or Handout 8.1 Capturing What Matters Most to Me
:05	My Commitments	Increase accountability, intention, and likelihood of successful goal attainment	• Handout 8.2 My Commitments
:05	Closing Circle	Complete the session	• Standing circle • Extinguish candles
:05	Logistics for next session	Ensure Group continuity and clarity of requirements for the next session	• Designate Group Guide, time, place • Choose a new Growth Buddy • Session Accelerator 9.1 Stuck Situation • Complete Brand of Me Collage

What You'll Need

- Poem
- Candle for each woman
- Digital timer
- Personal journal or notebook
- Calendar for setting next session's date
- Materials: 11 x14 poster paper, markers, colored pens, magazines, scissors, glue
- Session Accelerator 8.1 What's the Evidence?
- Session Accelerator 8.2 Collage of Possibilities
- Handout 8.1 Capturing What Matters Most to Me
- Handout 8.2 My Commitments
- Session Accelerator 9.1 Stuck Situation

Session Accelerator and handouts are provided as downloadable files at www.WomenConnected.com

What Happens During "The Brand of Me" Session

0:0 WELCOME (5 MINUTES)

Prior to starting the group, place a candle for each woman near the location where the group will be gathered. Each woman will light a candle at the end of her Check-In.

Group Guide welcomes the group to her home and this session.

We'll begin by taking three or four deep breaths. As you inhale, breathe deeply into all the possibilities waiting to be discovered. As you exhale, sink deeply into your authentic self and relax into a state of openness and connection to all that you are meant to be, and be present to new possibilities and discoveries.

Group Guide reads her preselected poem.

After the poem is read say:
Silently affirm to yourself the intention you're holding for this session. How will you show up for today's session, what will you contribute, and how will you demonstrate your support to the group?

Allow one minute of quiet reflection and then proceed to Check-In.

0:05 CHECK-IN (20 MINUTES)

Let's begin our Check-In. Each person has two to three minutes to share her thoughts on the following topics:

- ☐ Begin by stating your purpose.
- ☐ Report the status of your last session's commitment.
- ☐ What I've learned about myself since our last session is . . .

Who would like to begin?

Remember that the Group Guide will model the time frame for Check-In. Tell the group that you'll be using the digital timer, and that when the two minutes are up, the next person to her right checks in. Be sure to stay within the two-minute time frame.

As each individual completes her Check-In, she lights a candle and states her intention for the session.

After Check-In is complete, proceed to the next activity. You might say something like:

Let's take a look at the Session Accelerator: What's the Evidence? to find out what you discovered about yourself.

0:25 WHAT'S THE EVIDENCE?
(10 MINUTES)

Instruct group to take out their completed Session Accelerator 8.1 and partner with Growth Buddy from last session.

We'll take 10 minutes (5 minutes per person) and discuss the evidence you collected to affirm the positive belief and disprove the negative belief about yourself. I'll be the timekeeper and let you know when five minutes are left for the activity to be complete.

Group Guide sets the digital time for five minutes.

After five minutes have passed, inform the group of the remaining time left to finish the activity and of

the need to switch speakers. Reset digital timer for five minutes.

At the end of five minutes, proceed to the Large Group Discussion.

0:35 WHAT'S THE EVIDENCE?
LARGE GROUP DISCUSSION (5 MINUTES)

- ☐ Who would like to share what she learned from this Session Accelerator: What's the Evidence?
- ☐ Did anyone have any surprises? What were they?

After several women have shared their thoughts, proceed to the focus of today's session.

0:40 INTRODUCTION TO THE BRAND
OF ME (5 MINUTES)

Today's session is The Brand of Me. We'll be exploring these questions:

- ☐ What is the current story that your life is telling the world?
- ☐ How do you want to represent yourself going forward?
- ☐ What are you in the process of becoming?

The purpose of this session is to create a collage which represents the unique gifts you bring to the world, who you are when you're at your best, and what you're intentionally bringing forward into the future.

It's also an opportunity to state how you want to be perceived by others. First, we'll share our Collage of Possibilities with a small group, and then we'll come together and individually create our Brand of Me Collages.

0:45 COLLAGE OF POSSIBILITIES (20 MINUTES)

Ask the group to take out their Collage of Possibilities (childhood photo on a poster with words and descriptive phrases).

Let's divide the group in half. Number off as follows: 1, 2, 1, 2, and so on. All the *ones* form one circle, and the *twos* form a separate circle.

Wait until the groups are formed and settled down, and then say:
Here is what we'll be discussing in our small groups:

☐ Each woman will share her Collage of Possibilities.
☐ Explain why you chose this particular childhood photo.
☐ What was possible for this child—spiritually, emotionally, financially, in her relationships, regarding her health, and anything else that occurs to you?
☐ Share any insights that you have related to the activity.

I'll be the timekeeper for the activity in my group. The other group needs to have a timekeeper to keep them on track. Who would like to volunteer to be the timekeeper? *(pause)* Thank you. Each woman has up to five minutes to share her thoughts.

When there are five minutes left for this activity, notify the group that they have five minutes to complete their conversation.

1:05 COLLAGE OF POSSIBILITIES LARGE GROUP DISCUSSION (5 MINUTES)

Group Guide leads a brief discussion on what was noticed, learned, or experienced during the Collage of Possibilities activity. Some possible questions to elicit discussion might be:

☐ What did you notice about yourself and others during this activity?
☐ What feelings were generated?
☐ Was it easy or hard? Why or why not?

Keep track of time and when five minutes have passed proceed to the next activity.

1:10 CREATING THE BRAND OF ME COLLAGE (55 MINUTES)

It's now time to take out the materials that you brought to create your own personal collage. *(Poster board, magazines, scissors, glue, colored pens, markers, and a current photo of yourself.)* As you create your collage, keep in mind the following:

- [ ] What is currently working in your life that you'd like to expand?
- [ ] Reflecting back on your vision and purpose, what do you want to create that is not currently present in your life?
- [ ] What is the story you want others telling about you and what you're about in life?

We will have up to one hour to create our Brand of Me Collages. For some, this will be enough time to complete the activity. Others will want to take it home and spend more time on it. Let's get started, and if you need anything, just holler!

Every now and then someone can't find the perfect photo to illustrate what her brand happens to be. If this happens, encourage her to ask the group for help. For example, "I'm looking for a picture of a woman exercising. If someone sees something I can use, let me know."

When there are 10 minutes remaining for this activity, inform the women so that they can begin to finish up and put away their materials. Assure them that they'll be able to finish their collages at home before the next session.

2:05 THE BRAND OF ME—LAST THOUGHTS (5 MINUTES)

At our next session we'll have the opportunity to share our Brand of Me Collages with the entire group. Speaking about our brand brings our desires and wishes out into the world. And in Women Connected, we'll continue to support one another in bringing our best selves forward in whatever we do.

2:10 CAPTURING WHAT MATTERS MOST TO ME (5 MINUTES)

Distribute Handout 8.1

We'll spend the next five minutes in silence to capture our thoughts and feelings about today's session. Please take out your personal journal or use the handout to capture what matters most from today's session.

As you journal about this session, you might ask yourself:
- ☐ What was most valuable to me in this session?
- ☐ How did it feel to spend time creating my own unique brand?
- ☐ What did I like most about the brand that I created?

I'll be the timekeeper and set the digital timer for five minutes.

When time is up you might ask:
Would anyone like to share one of her comments with the group?

Take a minute or two and listen to a few comments, and then continue on to the next activity.

2:15 MY COMMITMENTS (5 MINUTES)

Distribute Handout 8.2

Take a moment and decide what you'd like to commit to between now and our next session. It's useful to think of a commitment aligned with creating your Brand or Future Perfect. It can be a small step that moves you in the direction of where you want to be at the end of this year. Revisit your 20 Dreams in Motion list. How is it going? Check to see if there are commitments you could initiate to move your dreams into reality. After we write our commitments, we'll each take a turn sharing our individual commitments with the group.

After everyone has written her commitments, say:
We'll take a few minutes and share our commitments with each other. Start by stating your commitment and why it is important to you at this time in your life. Who would like to go first?

After the last person has shared her commitments, thank the group and proceed to the Closing Circle.

2:20 CLOSING CIRCLE (5 MINUTES)

As we come to the end of this session, let's stand and form a circle. Take a moment to think of a word or brief thought that expresses what you experienced today in the Brand of Me session.

Rotating around the Circle, each woman shares her word or thoughts. After everyone has shared in Closing Circle, say:
This session is complete. Please extinguish your candle until we connect again.

2:25 WHAT'S NEXT—BREAKING THROUGH OBSTACLES (5 MINUTES)

Ask for a volunteer to be the Group Guide for the next session. Remind the group that each group member will take on the role of Group Guide at least once; by now some women will be volunteering for their second time. Ask everyone to take out her calendar to find an available date for the next session.

Our next session will be hosted by *(Group Guide)*, on *(date)*, at *(Group Guide's home)*, beginning promptly at *(time)*.

The topic will be Breaking Through Obstacles. In order to prepare for this session and maximize our time together, there will be a Session Accelerator: Stuck Situation. It will take approximately 20 to 30 minutes to complete. *(Pass out Session Accelerator 9.1.)* Bring your completed Brand of Me collage to our next session so we can share them during Check-In.

Choose a new Growth Buddy and decide when you'll be connecting for the first time.

Afterthoughts

Wasn't that fun? Making collages with Women Connected is one of my favorite things to do! It's not often that women give themselves time to play, be creative, cut and paste pictures, and laugh for no particular reason. And yet, the making of collages is a powerful and intentional process. You now have a visual representation of how you see yourself going forward. Rich colors, gorgeous photographs, and significant words have all come together to form a collage that expresses what is uniquely you. The Brand of Me Collage is a touchstone to keep you connected to what matters most in your life.

A couple of times a year I'll create a collage for myself, focusing on what I want to pay attention to during the next year. Last year I created a collage designed to support me in being bold. I had a great time cutting out words and pictures that represented power, strength, and boldness. As I was creating it, I thought about all the bold things I could initiate, how I would show up as a bold woman, what I would say, my tone of voice, my posture, and my bold presence. Just making the collage made me feel much bolder! I placed the collage in a prominent place in my office, and moved it to different locations around the room a couple of times a month. I've noticed that if I don't change my surroundings, after a while I don't notice what's there. Sometimes two months will go by before I change my office calendar! In fact, the calendar is a month behind right now. Does that ever happen to you? Anyway, I highly recommend intentionally bringing more fun and creativity into your life. It feels good—and that feeling-good energy is contagious!

To be born a girl is a gift we were given.
To become a real woman of wisdom and courage is
a gift we give the world.

☐ MARIANNE WILLIAMSON

Handout 8.1

CAPTURING WHAT MATTERS MOST TO ME

☐　What was most valuable to me in this session?

☐　How does it feel to spend time on creating my own unique brand?

☐　What do I like most about the brand that I've created?

Handout 8.2

MY COMMITMENTS

How we spend our days is, of course,
how we spend our lives.

☐ ANNIE DILLARD

Today's Date _____

Commitment _____
_____
_____

Date completed _____

Commitment _____
_____
_____

Date completed _____

Commitment _____
_____
_____

Date completed _____

Session Accelerator 9.1
STUCK SITUATION

As much as I want to be happy, feel good, and make my dreams come true, every now and then an obstacle shows up and slows me down. And sometimes the obstacle seems impossible to overcome. Just thinking about it can create anxiousness and tightness in my body. By now you've probably experienced how much wisdom is available to you and others in your Women Connected group. During the next session, Breaking Though Obstacles, you'll be introduced to a new approach for tackling the obstacles in your life so you can act on the wisdom available to you. There will be several opportunities in the session to learn from one another's experiences and to access the wisdom available in the group.

Think about two situations where you currently feel the most stuck. These might be situations in your life where an obstacle exists and you've been unable to move through it. Select situations in which, if the obstacles were removed, your life would work better. You may even know what needs to be done, and still you can't get unstuck. Briefly describe the situation, and write what you have done up to now.

EXAMPLE: Jane's 15-year-old son is a slob. He leaves his stuff everywhere, and thinks nothing of leaving dirty dishes and half-eaten meals wherever he took his last bite. She's tried everything she can think of to correct this problem. His room is a disaster, and she is tired of the on-going battle to get him to clean up his messes. Jane doesn't know what to do to fix the problem, and she feels stuck.

ANOTHER EXAMPLE: Last year I decided that I wanted to take a yoga class twice a week. I felt that the deep breathing exercises and stretching would be good for my health and fitness. I signed up for the class, purchased a special value packet of 10 sessions, and after two classes I didn't return. Something always came up in my schedule that took priority. I want to go to yoga and I don't make the time. I'm stuck.

Breaking Through

Obstacles

Keep on beginning and failing.
Each time you fail, start all over again, and you will grow
stronger until you have accomplished a purpose—
not the one you began with perhaps, but one you'll be glad
to remember.

□ ANNIE SULLIVAN

Dozens of books have been written on tackling obstacles, facing fears, and overcoming limiting beliefs. Some focus on the "feel the fear and do it anyway" approach, while others delve into the complexity of the topic and explore past experiences, traumas, and unhappy childhoods. However we approach it, though, the bottom line is this: breaking through any obstacle, large or small, takes commitment and willingness to change current belief structures. As we all know, this can be tough to do. The culprit behind almost every obstacle in our lives is fear. Fear can show up in many ways: fear of failure, fear of rejection, fear of appearing foolish, and fear of the unknown are among the most common varieties. I'm certain that you and your friends could add to this list. Astronaut Sally Ride spoke from experience when she said, "All adventures, especially into new territory, are scary."

But this time it's different—because

you're not alone. Women Connected is designed to provide you with group support and accountability practices that help tackle the obstacles preventing you from achieving your Future Perfect. And as Marcia Wieder, author of *Making Your Dreams Come True*, reminds us: "Commitment is a much more powerful way of living than waiting around and hoping, or worse, never doing anything to make your dreams happen."

When I was a single parent, I seemed to be constantly searching for ways to earn more money. As a high school teacher, my salary barely kept my kids and me afloat. One of my big dreams was to go to graduate school. I wanted to learn more, advance my career, and increase my income. When I received the graduate school application, I immediately went to work and gathered all the required information: undergraduate transcripts, test scores, letters of recommendation, and a current résumé. There was only one thing left to do: the college wanted a letter from me describing who I was, listing my educational goals, giving my assessment of the current state of education, and stating why I thought I'd be a good candidate for the program. Space in the program was limited, there would be hundreds of applicants, and it was important for the college to know more about me than merely my grades and test scores.

The deadline was approaching, and the letter became a huge obstacle in my mind. I didn't know what to say or how to start, and I was afraid that I wouldn't be good enough or smart enough to be accepted. One evening a couple of weeks before the deadline, I shared my fears with my women's group. I was so stuck that I was on the verge of letting go of my dream of attending graduate school—all because my fears were preventing me from writing a letter! My dear friend Susan had an idea. She would bring her tape recorder to my house, engage in a dialogue with me, and interview me for graduate school. With the help of her open-ended questions and curious mind, I was able to forget my fears. I got unstuck and the answers to her questions flowed out of me. Within an hour I had all the information I needed for the letter, and I had broken through an obstacle that might have kept me from realizing my dreams. Two months later my women's group had a big celebration when I received my graduate school acceptance letter. Without the support of my group and Susan's guidance, I might not have got past my fears of not being good enough or smart enough; I might not have managed to write the kind of letter that got me into graduate school.

During this session you'll identify internal and external obstacles that you are currently facing in your life. A Wisdom Blast, which is a solution-based activity, will give everyone the opportunity to expand her thinking and try out new strategies in dealing with obstacles. For any type of movement to take place, energy is needed. When we get stuck our energy is affected, and obstacles can seem impossible to get through. Harnessing the wisdom and experience of the group will create a renewed sense of energy and create the movement necessary to break through your obstacles. Are you ready? Let's get started!

Words of Wisdom

USE YOUR IMAGINATION

When you imagine yourself breaking through an obstacle, you take an important step in eliminating it from your life. Describe the obstacle in enough detail that it seems tangible.

☐ What does it look like?

☐ How does it feel?

☐ If it had a voice, what would it be saying?

Then imagine what your life would look like without the obstacle.

☐ How are things different now?

☐ What is happening?

☐ How do you feel?

☐ What are you saying to yourself about the success you've experienced in breaking through the obstacle?

MAKE IT REAL!

If the obstacle is internal, give it a physical form. For example, write a letter describing the internal obstacle or choose an object that represents it. A visual representation of the obstacle helps to bring it out into the open and out of the hidden corners of your mind. Then you can do something with it! A letter can be burned, crunched up, thrown away, or tossed into the sea. The same thing can be done with almost any object. This process can symbolically represent that you—not the obstacle—are in charge of your life.

Bumps in the Road—With Solutions!
INTERNAL CONVERSATIONS ARE KEEPING YOU STUCK

You notice that your internal conversations undermine and limit your ability to move through the obstacles in your life.

Solution: Find a trusted friend to whom you can describe the inner dialog that prevents you from doing what you want to do. After you've discussed what isn't working, share with your friend what you would rather be doing. Enlist her support and create a series of small steps that will help you move through the obstacle in the direction of possibility and success. Even the smallest movement counts!

TRY A CREATIVE APPROACH

You've tried everything you know and still seem unable to move through the obstacle.

Solution: Ask your Women Connected coaching group for a Wisdom Blast. This process will provide you with new strategies and options for eliminating the obstacle. Harnessing the wisdom and experience of wise women can create miracles in your life.

WISDOM BLAST DOESN'T ALLEVIATE YOUR OBSTACLE

The Wisdom Blast is fun and energizing, but doesn't help you with your long-standing and deep-seated obstacle.

Solution: You may be right. Some obstacles require a lifetime of healing and work to overcome. However, a Wisdom Blast can help you see things from different perspectives and sometimes gives you an unexpected boost.

Jennifer's Story

A gourmet chef with a passion for entertaining, Jennifer is a voracious reader in her mid-30s who loves big dogs and eclectic music. She has beautiful green eyes that really draw you in. In her Women Connected group, Jennifer learned that dreaming big can help you overcome even an apparently insurmountable obstacle.

When Jennifer came up with her 20

Dreams in Motion list, two of her biggest dreams—things that seemed impossible to her—were to become a runner and to own her own home. Within six months, she had already achieved both of these "impossible" dreams; she had a regular running routine and had purchased a house! She and her Growth Buddy, Stephanie, also a runner, decided that an even greater stretch would be to train for a triathlon. There was one obstacle: Jennifer didn't know how to swim. In fact, she was terrified of putting her face in the water. But she knew that with the support of Women Connected she could do it, so she began to make small steps toward her goal.

First she checked out the time schedule for her local pool. One day while running, Jennifer and Stephanie stopped at the pool and they noticed about 30 people swimming in six different lanes, filling the water. A woman who appeared to be coaching the swimmers noticed the two women watching, walked over, and asked if they needed help. Jennifer and Stephanie confessed they had a dream of doing a triathlon, but that Jennifer was afraid of the water. The coach said, "I teach swimming. Here's my card, and I guarantee that in one lesson I can give you an experience that will make you want to continue."

Jennifer put off calling for a month.

In the meantime, she created more small, doable steps: she bought a swimsuit, a swim cap, and goggles. Finally, she called and made an appointment for her first swim lesson. On the big day her Growth Buddy, Stephanie, came with her, and with Stephanie's welcome support, Jennifer took her first swim lesson. After that, the two took swimming lessons together for five months—at five in the morning, twice a week before work! After Jennifer had taken lessons for a while, the two women entered separate triathlons. Jennifer's event required her to swim a half-mile in open water. Although a year ago she had been terrified to put her face in the pool, Jennifer recently told me, "I just *love* swimming!"

The Big Picture: Breaking Through Obstacles

Suggested Time Frames	Activity	Purpose	Materials | Set-up
:05	Opening	Welcome; transition into Women Connected; become present	• Poem
:20	Check-In	Update, reconnect, report	• Candle for each woman • My Purpose statement
:35	Brand of Me collages	Present each person's brand to the group and connect with what's possible	• Completed Brand of Me collage
1:10	Session: Breaking Through Obstacles	Identify internal and external obstacles that prevent you from being successful in achieving goals, completing commitments, and creating a Future Perfect	• Completed Session Accelerator 9.1 Stuck Situation • Personal journal
:04 per person	Wisdom Blast	Access the group's wisdom	• Handout 9.1 Wisdom Blast • Paper and pen • Scribe • Timekeeper
:05	Capturing What Matters Most to Me	Highlight session insights that are most relevant to your life	• Personal journal or Handout 9.2 Capturing What Matters Most to Me
:05	My Commitments	Increase accountability, intention, and likelihood of successful goal attainment	• Handout 9.3 My Commitments
:05	Closing Circle	Complete the session	• Standing circle • Extinguish candles
:05	Logistics for next session	Ensure Group continuity and clarity of requirements for the next session	• Designate Group Guide, time, place • Choose a new Growth Buddy • Session Accelerator 10.1 My Courageous Conversation

What Happens During the "Breaking Through Obstacles" Session

0:00 WELCOME (5 MINUTES)

Prior to starting the group, place a candle for each woman near the location where the group will be gathered. Each woman will light a candle at the end of her Check-In.

Group Guide welcomes the group to her home and this session.

We'll begin by taking three to four deep breaths. As you inhale, breathe deeply into all the possibilities waiting to be discovered. As you exhale, sink deeply into your authentic self, relax into a state of openness and connection to self, and be present to new possibilities.

Group Guide reads her preselected poem.

After the poem is read say:

Silently affirm to yourself the intention you're holding for this session. How will you show up for today's session, what will you contribute, and how will you demonstrate your support to the group?

Allow one minute of quiet reflection and then proceed to Check-In.

What You'll Need
- Poem
- Candle for each woman
- Digital timer
- Personal journal or notebook
- Calendar for setting next session's date
- Brand of Me Collage
- Session Accelerator 9.1 Stuck Situation
- Handout 9.1 Wisdom Blast
- Handout 9.2 Capturing What Matters Most to Me
- Handout 9.3 My Commitments
- Session Accelerator 10.1 My Courageous Conversation

Session Accelerator and handouts are provided as downloadable files at www.WomenConnected.com

0:05 CHECK-IN (20 MINUTES)

Let's begin our Check-In. Each person has two to three minutes to share her thoughts on the following topics:

☐ Begin by stating your purpose.

☐ Report the status of your last session's commitment.

☐ What I learned about myself since our last session is . . .

Who would like to begin?

Remember that the Group Guide will model the time frame for Check-In. Tell the group that you'll be using the digital timer, and that when the two minutes are up, the next person to her right checks in. Be sure to stay within the two-minute time frame.

As each individual completes her Check-In, she lights a candle and states her intention for the session.

After Check-In is completed proceed to the next activity.

0:25 BRAND OF ME COLLAGES (30 MINUTES)
Invite the group to take out their Brand of Me Collages.

You have 30 minutes for this activity. Count the number of women in the group and divide this number into 30. This will give you the minutes available for each person to share her collage.

Before we begin this session, Breaking Through Obstacles, we'll spend time sharing the Brand of Me Collages that we started during our last session. Each of us will have a total of *(number)* minutes to present our brand to the group.

Let's see, who should go first? How about the woman who is the tallest? Then the woman on her left will go next, and we'll continue until everyone has shared her brand. I'll be the timekeeper, and when the time is up the next person will share her brand. Any questions? *(pause)* Let's begin.

Group Guide sets digital timer to the agreed upon number of minutes per person for this activity.

0:55 BRAND OF ME—LARGE GROUP DISCUSSION (5 MINUTES)
After everyone has shared her Brand of Me Collage, the Group Guide facilitates a brief discussion. You might want to consider using the following questions:

- [ ] What did you experience during this activity?
- [ ] How does it feel to hear about each other's brands?
- [ ] What does this activity make possible as we move into the focus of today's session, Breaking Through Obstacles?

When the discussion is complete, proceed to the next activity.

1:00 INTRODUCTION TO BREAKING THROUGH OBSTACLES (5 MINUTES)

Today's session is Breaking Through Obstacles. The purpose of this session is to identify internal and external obstacles that prevent us from accomplishing our vision, expressing our purpose, and achieving our dreams. During the session we'll join together and find solutions that will generate movement in the direction of all that we hold possible for ourselves.

This activity has three parts. During the first part we'll meet in a large group and generate a list of internal and external obstacles. We'll also spend time journaling our thoughts regarding the obstacles in our lives. During the second part of the activity we'll be working with a partner, discussing the Session Accelerator: Stuck Situation. The third and last part of this activity will be a Wisdom Blast, in which each of us will be given advice from the group on how to eliminate her obstacles.

1:05 NAME THAT INTERNAL OBSTACLE!
LARGE GROUP ACTIVITY (5 MINUTES)

Obstacles generally fall into two distinct areas. We'll first take a look at the internal obstacles of our lives. These are the ones that are self-imposed and put limits on what we do and how we behave. They include our self-critic, the negative voices in our head, and the myths about ourselves that get in the way of fulfilling our dreams. Together, let's make a list of all the internal obstacles that get in the way of completing commitments, achieving goals, and making dreams come true. What does your internal voice say when it's creating obstacles? An example of the internal voice might be, "I'm not smart enough to go to college" or "I'm too old to learn a new job."

Who would like to volunteer to list the internal obstacles generated from the group?

Group Guide facilitates the listing of internal obstacles and then posts the list in a visible location in the room.

After five minutes proceed to the next part of this process.

1:10 JOURNALING—INTERNAL OBSTACLES (5 MINUTES)

Take out your personal journal and select one of your frequently-occurring internal obstacles. For the next several minutes describe your feelings regarding this obstacle. You may respond to the following questions or simply write what is on your mind, related to this specific obstacle.

☐ How has it limited you?
☐ How has it served you?
☐ What has it taught you?
☐ Are you ready to release it?

Group Guide sets digital timer for five minutes.

After five minutes, proceed to the next part of this process by saying:

Please finish your last thoughts. It is time to explore the external obstacles in our lives.

1:15 NAME THAT EXTERNAL OBSTACLE! LARGE GROUP ACTIVITY (5 MINUTES)

Other types of obstacles are more external in nature. External obstacles show up as people or situations that we don't have control over, and that prevent us from getting to where we want to go. For example, a boss at work, a significant other, a child, the economy, or even the weather can act as an external obstacle in your life. Together, let's generate a list of as many external obstacles as we can think of. Who would like to volunteer to list the external obstacles that the group generates?

Group Guide facilitates the listing of external obstacles and then posts the list in a visible location in the room.

After five minutes proceed to the next part of this process.

1:20 JOURNALING—EXTERNAL OBSTACLES (5 MINUTES)

Once again, please take out your journal and select one of your frequently-occurring external obstacles. As you write about this external obstacle in your journal, keep in mind the following questions:

- ☐ How has it limited you?
- ☐ Are you ready to do something about it?
- ☐ What will you gain by letting it go?

Group Guides sets digital timer for five minutes.

At the end of five minutes say:
Take a moment to finish your last thought.

We've generated quite a list of obstacles, haven't we? Please find a partner for the next part of this activity.

Wait until everyone has a partner, and then continue with the directions.

1:25 STUCK SITUATION (10 MINUTES)
Instruct the group to take out their completed Session Accelerator 9.1.

Describe the stuck situation to your partner. Discuss two or three obstacles that are keeping you stuck. Then identify the one obstacle whose absence would most likely allow you to move forward in your stuck situation. Each partner will have five minutes, and I'll let you know when to switch speakers.

Group Guide sets digital timer for five minutes.

After five minutes ask the group to switch speakers, and let them know that they have five minutes left to complete their discussion. Group Guide resets digital timer for five minutes.

At the end of the five minutes, say:
It's time for the last part of this activity.

1:35 WISDOM BLAST (35 MINUTES)
Distribute Handout 9.1

There are 35 minutes left for this activity. If you have eight women in the group, each woman will experience a four-minute Wisdom Blast. This time includes sharing the obstacle that she wants to eliminate from her life. If you have more or less time available for this activity, divide the available time by the number of women in your group to determine how much time each woman will have for her Wisdom Blast.

We've spent time identifying and exploring our internal and external obstacles. Now we'll share our knowledge and experience with one another to explore ways to eliminate these obstacles from our lives. Each person will have *(number)* minutes for the Wisdom Blasts. When it's your turn, you'll briefly describe the stuck situation and the number-one obstacle you are currently facing. The group's role is to find a solution to the problem. Keep the solutions brief.

When it is your turn for a Wisdom Blast, your role is to listen without censoring. Our role is to give our best advice to you. When your time is up, take the paper that has your solutions on it. Growth Buddies will take notes for each other during their Wisdom Blast. After you have received the list of solutions from your Growth Buddy, look over the list and pick one solution that you believe might work. Try out this solution before the next session and see what happens. You will be reporting back on your progress.

Some examples of obstacles that could be brought forth in a Wisdom Blast are:

- ☐ Lack of commitment to exercise
- ☐ Resistance to new ideas and to change
- ☐ Negative self-talk
- ☐ Fear of disappointing others

Let's get started. Today the person with the most freckles goes first.

Group Guide will be the timekeeper for the Wisdom Blast, unless someone else volunteers.

At the end of the Wisdom Blast, say something like:
We've generated a lot of information during this session and discovered creative solutions that we'll want to remember.

2:10 CAPTURING WHAT MATTERS MOST TO ME (5 MINUTES)
Distribute Handout 9.2

We'll spend the next five minutes in silence to capture our thoughts and feelings about this session. Please take out your personal journal or use the handout to capture what matters most from today's session.

As you journal about this session, you might ask yourself:

- ☐ What was most valuable to me in this session?
- ☐ How did the Wisdom Blast assist me in this session?
- ☐ How am I feeling in this moment?

I'll be the timekeeper and set the digital timer for five minutes.

When time is up you might ask:
Would anyone like to share one of their comments with the group?

Take a minute or two and listen to a few comments, then proceed to the next activity.

2:15 MY COMMITMENTS (5 MINUTES)

Distribute Handout 9.3

Take a moment and decide what you'd like to commit to between now and our next session. It might be useful to think of a commitment that would be aligned with creating your Future Perfect. It can be a small step that moves you in the direction of where you want to be at the end of this year.

After everyone has written their commitments, say: We'll take a few minutes and share our commitments with each other. Start by stating your commitment and why it is important to you at this time in your life. Who would like to go first?

After the last person has shared her commitments, thank the group and proceed to the Closing Circle.

2:20 CLOSING CIRCLE (5 MINUTES)

As we come to the end of this session, let's stand and form a circle. Take a moment and think of a word or brief thought that expresses what you experienced in the Breaking Through Obstacles session.

Rotating around the Circle, each woman shares her word or thoughts. After everyone has shared in Closing Circle, say:

This session is complete. Please extinguish your candle until we connect again.

2:25 WHAT'S NEXT—COURAGEOUS CONVERSATIONS (5 MINUTES)

Ask for a volunteer to be the Group Guide for the next session. Remind the group that each group member will take on the role of Group Guide at least once, and by now some women will be volunteering for their second time. Ask everyone to take out her calendar to find an available date for the next session.

Our next session will be hosted by *(Group Guide)*, on *(date)*, at *(Group Guide's home)*, beginning promptly at *(time)*.

The topic of the next session is Courageous Conversations. In order to prepare for this session and maximize our time together, please complete the Session Accelerator: My Courageous Conversations prior to our next session. It will take approximately 30 minutes to complete. *(Pass out Session Accelerator 10.1.)*

Choose a new Growth Buddy and decide when you will be connecting for the first time.

Afterthoughts

Obstacles are a part of life. I don't believe that anyone in the world has an obstacle-free life—even if she lives alone in a cave! As we acquire more wisdom, we become better able to manage obstacles as they show up, instead of letting the obstacles manage us. I have discovered that the more vocal I can be about the obstacle, shining a spotlight on it, the more easily I'm able to access my wisdom and the wisdom of others in order to move through it. It's a never-ending process. Just when I think I've got a handle on an obstacle, guess what? Another one shows up! But isn't that what personal growth is all about? As long as we're fully alive and continually learning, we'll be dealing with obstacles—and learning to manage them so they don't keep us from realizing our dreams. We can envision obstacles as stepping stones with which we build the path to the life we desire.

It's worth noting that many of the obstacles in our lives involve others; specifically, the conversations we haven't had with them. Our next session, Courageous Conversations, explores and provides frameworks for having specific conversations that, for whatever reason, we've put off, not had, or find impossible to initiate. These are conversations that are incomplete; thus, when addressed, they allow us to free up energy that can be dedicated to the creation of our dreams.

> Alone we can do so little—
> together we can do so much!
>
> ☐ HELEN KELLER

Handout 9.1

WISDOM BLAST

This process is designed to access the group's collective wisdom. It is a brainstorming session, and any idea is worth listening to. Sometimes the best ideas come out of left field! Each woman will have a designated number of minutes to briefly share her number-one obstacle and receive free-flowing advice from the group.

The role of the group is to stay focused, with the intention of providing solutions to the problem described. The role of the recipient is to listen, without comment or judgments. Just stay present, focused, and open to receiving the wisdom from the group.

All ideas will be captured for the recipient by her Growth Buddy. Before the next session, look over this list and choose what you believe to be the best solution to your obstacle. Try out the solution and report back to the group during the next Check-In.

Handout 9.2

CAPTURING WHAT MATTERS MOST TO ME

☐   What was most valuable to me in this session?

☐   How did the Wisdom Blast assist me in this session?

☐   How am I feeling in this moment?

Something which we think is impossible now,
is not impossible in another decade.

☐ CONSTANCE BAKER MOTLEY

Today's Date _____

Commitment _____
_____
_____

Date completed _____

Commitment _____
_____
_____

Date completed _____

Commitment _____
_____
_____

Date completed _____

Session Accelerator 10.1
MY COURAGEOUS CONVERSATION

INSTRUCTIONS

Use the following Courageous Conversation Model to describe a conversation that you'd like to initiate. Choose a conversation that you're concerned about having, one in which there is some fear attached to the outcome or to how the other person might respond. This conversation could be about anything from a piece of information that you chose not to share and you keep wondering if you should have, to an issue you are having in a relationship. It might be a concern that you've had but haven't expressed about one of your family members or children. It could be something that, if directly discussed, might move a relationship from being stuck or strained and create an opening for change and new actions. This is the perfect opportunity to contemplate and begin to prepare for that conversation.

On a sheet of paper or in your personal journal, using the Courageous Conversation Model, briefly describe the conversation you'd like to initiate. It is not necessary to go into great detail or describe the past. For example: "I'd like to have a conversation with my husband to discuss our finances. I feel like I've been over-spending, and I've been afraid to bring up the issue and my behavior." Another conversation might be with a neighbor: "I feel like the only time she calls me is to ask for a favor. We used to talk on a regular basis and do things together. I wonder if she still wants to be friends, because it's been feeling one-sided for a long time."

COURAGEOUS CONVERSATION MODEL

☐ Identify and state the issue. *(Isolate it from all the other issues, and choose one, and only one, issue for this conversation.)*

☐ What prevents me from initiating this conversation? *(List all the reasons and excuses that have prevented the conversation from taking place.)*

☐ What is the current impact on me? *(Time, energy expended, feelings, etc.)*

☐ What is the possible long-term impact on the relationship if this conversation doesn't take place?

☐ Predict what the other person might say.

☐ What would be the ideal outcome of this conversation?

A SAMPLE COURAGEOUS CONVERSATION

☐ Identify and state the issue. (Isolate it from all the other issues, and choose one, and only one, issue for this conversation.)

I want to have a discussion with my husband regarding our finances and my lack of responsibility in keeping my spending within our means.

☐ What prevents me from initiating this conversation? (List all the reasons and excuses that have prevented the conversation from taking place.)

I'm afraid that if I tell him I've been using my credit card, he'll get angry. I am worried that he'll want me to change my spending habits. I'm concerned that he will think I'm selfish and not interested in our financial future.

☐ How does not having this conversation affect me? (Time, energy expended, feelings, etc.)

I've been preoccupied with this issue, and each time I'm with my husband I think about telling him about my spending, but I don't. I get a knot in my stomach whenever I think about having the conversation. I feel like I am out of integrity and living a lie.

☐ What is the possible long-term impact on the relationship if this conversation doesn't take place?

If I'm dishonest in the financial area, I could easily become dishonest in other areas of our life. Barriers could come between us from the lack of honest and open communication. Our financial future could be jeopardized and we could end up without money for retirement.

☐ Predict what the other person might say.

How could you be so selfish? Why didn't you tell me? Don't you care about our financial future? You've placed a huge burden on me. Or, thank you for being honest. I know that this must have been difficult for you.

☐ What would be the ideal outcome of this conversation?

It wasn't as difficult as I had imagined. My husband was very understanding and forgiving. Together we are going to work on a financial plan and have a fresh start. I feel so much better and less guilty. I'm feeling more in love with my husband and feel closer to him as a result of our conversation.

Courageous
Conversations

> While no single conversation is guaranteed to change the trajectory of a career, a company, a relationship, or a life—any single conversation can.
>
> □ SUSAN SCOTT

Have you ever had something you wanted to say to someone, and didn't say it? Have you ever found yourself not speaking up about something that really matters to you? Is there a conversation you've been putting off until the right time, but then the right time never seems to arrive? Do you find yourself procrastinating about telling a friend what isn't working in your relationship, and how you want it to be different? Have you found yourself making excuses to keep from having a conversation you know needs to take place?

If you've said *yes* to any of these questions, then this session will support you in taking action. It might even change your life. At the very least, this session will free up the energy you've been using in thinking about (and avoiding) this conversation. By now, along with the other women in your Women Connected group, you've already discovered life-affirming ways to put this newfound energy to good use.

There have been countless times in my life when I couldn't muster the courage to say what I knew needed to be said, and I chickened out. I have been very creative in designing excuses that put off or delayed the inevitable difficult conversation. I tell myself it's not the right time. I'm not feeling strong enough or happy enough or confident enough. Or better yet, the other person is not happy enough, strong enough, or ready to have the conversation! You get the picture.

In my work with women, I have witnessed again and again that when we don't have those conversations we know in our hearts are necessary, we lose energy and begin to experience barriers arising between ourselves and others.

Sometimes it really is impossible to have the conversation you want and need to have with someone. For safety's sake, women who have been physically or emotionally abused are often unable to say what they want to say directly to their abuser. Maybe the one you need to talk to is no longer living, or their whereabouts are unknown. Don't be discouraged; it is still possible to say what needs to be said to someone or something that acts as a stand-in for the person who is not present.

In the 1970s I moved from California to Washington State. I had completed my two-year degree and wanted to continue my education. Out-of-state tuition was exorbitant, and I needed to wait a year to establish residency. During that year, I took several workshops that focused on self-esteem issues and personal development. One of these workshops had a profound

effect on me and led me to take more psychology classes once I returned to college. In this workshop I had the opportunity to have a conversation with my dad, who had passed away many years before. The technique used was called empty chair, and it originated in Gestalt therapy. Two chairs were placed in the center of a circle of people. I sat in one chair and imagined I faced my dad in the empty chair. With encouragement from the facilitator, I said all the things I had wanted to say to my dad. I shared my grief, my anger at being abandoned by him, and all the things his death at such an early age prevented us from doing together. As you can imagine it was a painful process, and yet at the end of our conversation, I felt a completeness I hadn't known since his death. Since then I have had many conversations using the empty chair technique—some alone, some with support from my women's group—and the result is usually the same. I feel better after speaking my thoughts and feelings.

Another useful technique is to write a letter to the person with whom you want to have the conversation. In some cases just the process of writing the letter is enough; in other cases the letter is mailed. Occasionally a woman discovers that after describing and discussing the unresolved issue or conversation that she wants to initiate, the issue is resolved and the need to have the courageous conversation disappears.

Whichever technique you choose will free up the energy you currently use in wondering if you should or shouldn't have the conversation. During this session you'll have the opportunity to work through a courageous conversation with the support and shared wisdom of Women Connected. It does make a difference—and I speak from lots of experience!

Words of Wisdom
DON'T POSTPONE DIFFICULT CONVERSATIONS

It's important to address issues in relationships as they arise, and to be as honest as possible in expressing your thoughts and feelings. From experience I have discovered that it's much easier to have a conversation when the issue is fresh, rather than waiting for the right time, place, mood, or level of confidence I think I need in order to initiate the conversation.

CONSERVE YOUR ENERGY

A conversation that seemed slightly difficult in the beginning becomes much more difficult with each delay—and each delay consumes more of your creative energies. Before you know it, this slightly difficult conversation has become one that takes courage.

Bumps in the Road—With Solutions!
STALL TACTICS

You notice that you're making up a lot of excuses and seem preoccupied with a conversation that you're not having with someone.

Solution: With the support of your Growth Buddy, set a time and place to do something. Either have the courageous conversation, or select another approach that will release you from the need to have the conversation.

THE NEVER-ENDING STORY

You keep rehearsing the conversation in your head, again and again and again.

Solution: Get it out of your head and write it down, or bring it to Women Connected, or talk to a trusted friend. Just get into action and do something about it.

TRIANGLES DON'T WORK!

You find yourself talking to other people about the individual with whom you want to have the conversation, yet you don't speak directly to that person.

Solution: Make a promise to yourself not to involve other people in the situation unless you're ready to do something about it.

RELATIONSHIPS IN JEOPARDY

Each time you see the person with whom you need to have a courageous conversation, you feel uncomfortable, and it's creating a distance in your relationship.

Solution: Remember that you are not alone. Ask your Women Connected group for support or advice. Then make a commitment to yourself to say what needs to be said to that person.

Tiffany's Story

Tiffany had delayed having a courageous conversation with her dad. Her parents had divorced when she was three years old, and for the next 15 years she had rarely seen him. Occasionally her father sent her a birthday card with a few dollars or a present at Christmas, but she had never had the father-daughter relationship she hoped for.

At 31, Tiffany was a successful third-grade teacher. Her big hearty laugh made her stand out in a crowd. An athlete all her life, she excelled in basketball and numerous other sports. In Women Connected, Tiffany discovered a strong desire to reach out to her dad. She wanted to get to know him, understand his world, and create a relationship with him. During Women Connected sessions Tiffany felt extremely anxious whenever she considered having this courageous conversation with her dad.

In one session Tiffany asked for the group's support. She rehearsed what she wanted to say, received feedback from the group, and arranged to have her Growth Buddy, Laurie, be present during the phone call to her dad. Laurie encouraged Tiffany, assuring her that she would be available for her before, during, and after the phone call. Tiffany eventually decided to place the call from Laurie's house. With her Growth Buddy's support, Tiffany told her dad she wanted him to be more involved in her life. Her father expressed sorrow that his life had not been structured around being a loving dad. Tiffany's father was happy she had called, saying that he had often longed to speak to her but had avoided contacting her out of fear that she might resent his long absence.

Today Tiffany and her father are creating a new relationship built on love and greater understanding. Although he lives 1500 miles away, they speak on the phone at least twice a month now, and her dad has offered to help her with the educational expense involved in seeking her master's degree in education. Tiffany credits her Women Connected group with providing the critical support that helped her move through her fears and gather the courage to have this life-changing conversation.

The Big Picture: Courageous Conversations

Suggested Time Frames	Activity	Purpose	Materials | Set-up
:05	Opening	Welcome; transition into Women Connected; become present	• Poem
:40	Check-In	Update, reconnect, report	• Candle for each woman • My Purpose statement
1:45	Session: Courageous Conversations	Free up blocked energy, change current status of a relationship, and stand up for oneself and face fears	• Completed Session Accelerator 10.1 My Courageous Conversation
:05	Capturing What Matters Most to Me	Highlight session insights that are most relevant to your life	• Personal journal or Handout 10.1 Capturing What Matters Most to Me
:05	My Commitments	Increase accountability, intention, and likelihood of successful goal attainment	• Handout 10.2 My Commitments
:05	Closing Circle	Complete the session	• Standing circle • Extinguish candles
:05	Logistics for next session	Ensure Group continuity and clarity of requirements for the next session	• Designate Group Guide, time, place • Choose a new Growth Buddy • Session Accelerator 11.1 Women Connected Acknowledgments and 20 Dreams in Motion

What You'll Need

- Poem
- Candle for each woman
- Digital timer
- Personal journal or notebook
- Calendar for setting next session's date
- Session Accelerator 10.1 My Courageous Conversation
- Handout 10.1 Capturing What Matters Most to Me
- Handout 10.2 My Commitments
- Session Accelerator 11.1 Women Connected Acknowledgments and 20 Dreams in Motion

Session Accelerator and handouts are provided as downloadable files at www.WomenConnected.com

What Happens During the "Courageous Conversations" Session

0:00 WELCOME (5 MINUTES)

Prior to starting the group, place a candle for each woman near the location where the group will be gathered. Each woman will light a candle at the end of her Check-In.

Group Guide welcomes the group to her home and this session.

Inform the group that there will be a couple minutes of silence. The purpose is to quiet the mind, get

present, and shift focus to intentional conversations.

We'll begin by taking three to four deep breaths. As you inhale, breathe deeply into all the possibilities waiting to be discovered. As you exhale, sink deeply into your authentic self. Relax into a state of openness and connection to self, staying present to new possibilities and conversations.

Group Guide reads her preselected poem.
After the poem is read say:

Silently affirm to yourself the intention you're holding for this session. How will you show up for today's session, what will you contribute, and how will you demonstrate your support to the group?

Allow one minute of quiet reflection and then proceed to Check-In.

0:05 CHECK-IN (40 MINUTES)

Please note that this is an extended Check-In to allow extra time for the update on obstacles.

Let's begin our Check-In. Each person has four to five minutes *(depending on the size of the group)* to share her thoughts on the following topics:

- Begin by stating your purpose.
- Report the status of your last session's commitments.
- Briefly report your progress in eliminating your obstacle. State the obstacle, the idea used from the Wisdom Blast, and the current status of the obstacle.

Who would like to begin?

Remember that the Group Guide will model the time frame for Check-In. Tell the group that you'll be using the digital timer and that each person will have (number) minutes. You have 40 minutes for this Check-In. Divide the number of people present into 40 to determine the exact number of minutes each woman has for her Check-In. The person to your right goes next.

As each individual completes her Check-In, she lights a candle and states her intention for the session.

After Check-In is completed, proceed to the next activity.

0:45 INTRODUCTION TO COURAGEOUS CONVERSATIONS (5 MINUTES)

The focus of this session is Courageous Conversations. This session is an opportunity for us to identify a specific conversation, practice the conversation with a partner, and then make a plan to initiate the conver-sation or decide that we no longer choose to engage in the conversation. This can be challenging work, and it also can move us closer to being more open and honest in the relationships that matter most to us. We'll be spending the next hour on this very important topic.

Choose a partner you would like to be with as you work through your Courageous Conversation.

Pause. Wait until everyone has a partner and then give the following directions.

0:50 MY COURAGEOUS CONVERSATION (20 MINUTES)

Ask the group to take out their completed Session Accelerator 10.1.

PARTNER ACTIVITY

During this activity each partner has 10 minutes to discuss the conversation she wrote about in her Session Accelerator. It is not necessary to go into great detail, just share what you'd like to say and why you haven't had the conversation yet. Pay attention to clarity. It is important to pick one thing to discuss, not to include a year's worth of baggage. If I want to discuss finances with my husband, I need to stick to that topic and not bring in stuff on other issues. I'll be the timekeeper and inform you when 10 minutes are left.

After 10 minutes, inform the group that half the time has passed and the second person can begin describing her conversation.

When a total of 20 minutes are up, get the group's attention for the next set of directions.

1:10 PRACTICE MAKES PERFECT—CONVERSATIONS IN MOTION (5 MINUTES)

Now that you've had a chance to discuss the Courageous Conversation, it's time to practice saying what you'd like to say—out loud—to your partner. Each of you will have 10 minutes to devote to your practice conversation. Decide who would like to go first. *(pause)* Raise your hand if you volunteered to go first. You'll be Partner A, and Partner B will pretend to be the person with whom you'll have the conversation.

COACH YOUR PARTNER

To start, Partner A will coach Partner B on the role she is playing, the reaction you would expect the other person to have, and anything else you can share with your partner to make it real for you as you practice the conversation. Please take a couple of minutes and do this now.

Keep track of time, and after two minutes give one more minute for the partners to finish their discussion.

We're almost ready to begin our practice conversations.

Before Partner A begins the conversation, I'd like all the As to bring your full attention and focus to this practice session. Take a long, deep breath, hold it, and release. Once again, take a deep breath, hold it, and release. Place your feet firmly on the ground, open up your heart space for connection, and be clear about why you are choosing to have this conversation. Be aware of your body and any sensations as you engage in the conversation.

Are there any questions? *(pause)*

Okay. Here are the steps in this process. Partner A will begin the conversation by stating the issue, the impact of not having the conversation, and the current status of the relationship. Then she will share how she would like the issue to be resolved. It might be helpful to refer to your Session Accelerator. You'll have five minutes to say whatever you need to say during this time.

Partner B's role is to listen deeply, support your partner by taking on the role fully, challenging her when appropriate, and noticing the tone of voice, body movements, and overall demeanor. You will provide feedback at the end of the conversation.

Things for Partner A to avoid while having the conversation:
- [ ] Name calling
- [ ] Blaming
- [ ] Accusations
- [ ] Arguing to support your point of view
- [ ] Increasing volume of voice

Remember that you want this conversation to change the status of this relationship. It is almost a guarantee that some movement will occur as a result of your courage in initiating this conversation.

1:15 PARTNER A'S COURAGEOUS CONVERSATION (5 MINUTES)
Please begin, and I will inform you when it is time to end the five-minute practice conversation.

Group Guide keeps track of time. After five minutes, inform the group that it is time for the next set of directions.

1:20 REVERSE ROLES (5 MINUTES)

It's now time to reverse roles. We'll continue with the same conversation. The first speaker, Partner A, will become the listener, and the first listener, Partner B, will take on the role of the original speaker. Partner B will speak the conversation as if she is Partner A. This will help you to understand the needs and feelings of each partner. It doesn't need to be perfect; do your best and remember that the more you practice the easier it will become. You'll have five minutes of practice with this portion of the activity.

After five minutes have passed, inform group that it is time to complete their conversations.

1:25 FEEDBACK FROM PARTNER (5 MINUTES)

Each partner shares her observations of the conversation. Provide feedback on tone of voice, body movements, and overall demeanor.

After five minutes, inform the group that it is time to move on to the next part of the activity.

1:30 PRACTICE MAKES PERFECT, CONTINUED (20 MINUTES)

We will now repeat the entire process—step by step—using Partner B's Courageous Conversation. Review each of the steps listed under the Practice Makes Perfect—Conversations in Motion section earlier in this chapter. Go through each of the steps as you did with Partner A's conversation. I'll inform the group when it is time to reverse roles in the conversation.

Group Guide keeps track of time during this activity. Set the digital timer for each segment and notify the partners when it's time to switch roles, and again when it's time to provide feedback to each other.

When the Bs have completed their conversations and the feedback has been shared between the partners, proceed to the group discussion of this activity.

1:50 COURAGEOUS CONVERSATIONS LARGE GROUP DISCUSSION (10 MINUTES)

Lead a brief discussion on this activity. A few suggested questions are:

- ☐ What was it like to practice the conversation with your partner?
- ☐ What did you notice about yourself and your partner during this activity?
- ☐ Was difficult? Why or why not?

It's now time to build some accountability into this process.

2:00 THE GAME PLAN
CONVERSATIONS IN ACTION (10 MINUTES)

Instruct the group to continue with the same partner during this activity. Each partner will have up to five minutes to discuss her commitment related to her Courageous Conversation.

Discuss with your partner when and how you'd like to initiate the courageous conversation.

Make a commitment to have the conversation by a specific date. Arrange a time to check in with your support partner before and after the conversation.

Group Guide keeps track of time. When five minutes are up, tell group to switch speakers. After 10 minutes, inform the group that time is up and move on to the next activity.

2:10 CAPTURING WHAT MATTERS MOST TO ME (5 MINUTES)
Distribute Handout 10.1

We'll spend the next five minutes in silence to capture our thoughts and feelings about this session. Please take out your personal journal or use the handout to capture what matters most from this session.

As you journal about this session, you might ask yourself:
- ☐ What did I find to be of most value in this session?
- ☐ How do I feel about having a Courageous Conversation?
- ☐ What will I do to make it happen?
- ☐ How will I feel when the conversation has been completed?

I'll be the timekeeper and set the digital timer for five minutes.

When time is up, you might ask:
Would anyone like to share one of their comments with the group?

Take a minute or two and listen to a few comments, then go on to the next activity.

2:15 MY COMMITMENTS (5 MINUTES)
Distribute Handout 10.2

Take a moment and decide what you'd like to commit to before our next session. Choose a commitment that moves you closer to completing some of the goals listed on your Dreams in Motion list. We'll be reporting our progress during our next

Check-In. After we write our commitments, we'll each take a turn and share them with the group.

After everyone has written her commitments, say:
We'll take a few minutes and share our commitments with each other. Start by stating your commitment and why it is important to you at this time in your life. Who would like to go first?

After the last person has shared her commitments, thank the group and proceed to the Closing Circle.

2:20 CLOSING CIRCLE (5 MINUTES)

As we come to the end of this session, it's time to form our Closing Circle. Take a moment and think of a word, brief thought, or experience that you'd like to share from the Courageous Conversation session.

Rotating around the Circle, each woman shares her word or thoughts. After everyone has shared in Closing Circle, say:
This session is complete. Please extinguish your candle until we connect again.

2:25 WHAT'S NEXT—CELEBRATING US! (5 MINUTES)

Ask for a volunteer to be the Group Guide for the last session. Ask everyone to take out her calendar to find an available date for the next session.

The next session will be hosted by *(Group Guide)*, on *(date)*, at *(Group Guide's home)*, beginning promptly at *(time)*.

Our next topic is Celebrating Us! Bring the completed Session Accelerator: Women Connected Acknowledgments to the next session. *(Pass out Session Accelerator 11.1.)*

Since the next session will be the formal completion of the Women Connected 11-Session Coaching Guide, we'll celebrate with a potluck meal. Who would like to volunteer to coordinate the food and beverages for our celebration meal?

Choose a new Growth Buddy and decide how you will connect with each other.

Afterthoughts

This session may have been a real challenge, and for some, not much fun at all. However, I hope you discovered that having a practice session with a trusted friend is a valuable technique to prepare you for the courageous conversations in your life. I encourage you to continue to use this strategy whenever the need arises—especially before the conversation goes from the uncomfortable stage to a stage that takes even more courage.

My well-worn thesaurus defines courage as "guts, nerve, daring, bravery, and audacity." That about sums it up, doesn't it? There is an upside to initiating the conversations that you find difficult. Over time you'll discover that choosing to engage in a courageous conversation brings with it some great benefits.

Every conversation that isn't taking place, for whatever reason, blocks energy that could be used elsewhere in your life. The degree to which you are not current or complete with the conversations in your life directly impacts the energy you have available to create new things. One of the big advantages to freeing blocked energy is that your available energy increases, and this freed energy will keep you moving forward toward your vision, your dreams, and a more fulfilling life.

Profound joy of the heart is like a magnet that indicates the path of life. One has to follow it, even though one enters into a way full of difficulties.

☐ MOTHER TERESA

Handout 10.1

CAPTURING WHAT MATTERS MOST TO ME

☐   What did I find to be of most value in this session?

☐   How do I feel about having a courageous conversation?

☐   What will I do to make it happen?

☐   How will I feel when the conversation has been completed?

I am like a falling star who has finally found her place next to another in a lovely constellation, where we will sparkle in the heavens forever.

□ AMY TAN

I love celebrations. Doesn't everyone? And there's plenty to celebrate: You've just completed your first Women Connected program! Give yourself a pat on the back and a big hug, and bask in the accomplishments of these last 10 sessions. As you look at yourself and those in your group, what do you see? Really look at their faces . . . I'll bet you've noticed that some of the women in your group look entirely different to you than they did during your initial Evening of Exploration. Women have reported feeling younger than when they started Women Connected, that they walk with a new spring in their step and experience a renewed sense of commitment to making their dreams come true. If you took a group photo at the first session, compare that photo to how you all look and feel now. Don't forget to take a photo during this session of celebration, as well. You'll want to remember this moment.

Several years ago I read a research survey designed to discover what made people happy at work. You might expect that being well paid would be the number one factor in job satisfaction; however, in a list of five factors, being well paid was fourth. First on the list was this: feeling acknowledged and appreciated by coworkers. In all my years of working with people, I have yet to hear someone say, "I get too many compliments; I am so tired of people telling me how wonderful I am and that I've made a difference in their lives."

As you move into this session, keep in mind that what we're celebrating is not just the completion of 11 Women Connected sessions. We are celebrating and acknowledging women who have moved through resistance to achieve their dreams, who have accomplished more than they thought possible, and who have been willing to be vulnerable and ask for help. We are celebrating, as well, the unique qualities each of you has brought to this group. For many of you it has been a life-changing experience, and one that you'll always remember.

Words of Wisdom
CELEBRATE WITH A MEAL
There is something about breaking bread together that contributes to the celebratory mood of this session. I suggest you make plans to have a potluck lunch or dinner. You might want to consider having a theme for the meal, preparing a variety of appetizers and salads, or even cooking something together. Whatever you decide, it will be absolutely perfect.

EXTEND THE TIME FOR THIS SESSION
This is a session where you'll want to savor each moment and not feel rushed at the end. I suggest leaving the digital timer at home! You'll want to add an additional hour for the meal. Typically this session will take three or four hours.

SPEND QUALITY TIME COMPLETING ACKNOWLEDGMENTS FOR EACH WOMAN
Give yourself plenty of time and quiet reflection for writing acknowledgments. Review your notes from each session; remember who said just the right thing at the right time, who supported you in special ways, and who opened up your thinking about a particular issue. It's important to give specific examples when acknowledging someone. A nice acknowledgement would be "I appreciate your support during our time in Women Connected." A heartfelt and powerful acknowledgment might sound like "When I was unable to ask for help in dealing with my son's depression, you noticed and helped me find a thera-

pist for him. I was stuck, and I'll be forever grateful for your support and friendship."

Here's another example of a nice acknowledgement: "I learned so much from you." Now notice the difference when you give specific details: "When you left your secure job and started your own business, I admired your courage and determination to make it on your own. As a result of seeing you complete this big dream, I realized it was possible for me to make a change in my life, too. Thank you so much for this gift."

TAKE THE TIME TO ACKNOWLEDGE YOURSELF

It is common for women to minimize their own accomplishments and feel more comfortable supporting and acknowledging others. You have spent many months of your life attending Women Connected coaching sessions, meeting with your Growth Buddies, and completing your commitments. Now is the time to acknowledge what you appreciate about your life and yourself. Don't be shy, be bold, and be proud of all that you've done and all that you intend to do.

TAPE RECORD THE ACKNOWLEDGMENT PROCESS

You'll probably want to listen again to all the wonderful acknowledgments shared in this session. It is such a powerful experience that you'll want to capture every moment.

Bumps in the Road—With Solutions!
A RELUCTANT PARTICIPANT

Someone is feeling uncomfortable and would rather watch the process.

Solution: As you know by now, Women Connected is not a spectator sport. This is no time to miss out on the benefits of participation. Listen to the concerns of the woman and gently encourage her to join in the process so the rest of the group can share their acknowledgments of her. For some it can be far more difficult to hear the good news about themselves than the bad. Remember, this process is part of Women Connected.

RUSHING THE PROCESS

You notice that some people seem to be rushing through the process of sharing their acknowledgments.

Solution: When it is your turn to give acknowledgments, set the pace; go slowly and encourage others to do the same. Ask the group to allow for a pause before delivering the next acknowledgment so everyone can take it in. Savor this time together.

NERVOUS ENERGY

One woman seems very anxious and nervous as she is receiving acknowledgments—and this woman could be you!

Solution: Take a deep breath, stay open, and ask for a moment so that you can quiet the chatter in your mind. If you don't, you might miss some of the richness of the experience.

Tina's Story

Sometimes part of Celebrating Us! is moving on and saying goodbye. When Tina's group said goodbye to her, she was leaving to move to an island in southeastern Alaska.

Strong and physically fit, with big green eyes and a heart as big as her new home state of Alaska, Tina is one of the most loving and thoughtful women I know. Four years ago she moved to Sitka, Alaska, with her husband, Keith. His dream had always been to fish, hunt, and be close to nature all year round. It was not a life that Tina had imagined for herself, and in the beginning she struggled to find her own way. Leaving her family and friends was painful. And yet she loved her husband deeply, and knew that in time she'd be able to create new dreams for herself in Sitka.

In Women Connected, Tina learned the importance of aligning her purpose and vision, of being intentional about communicating her dreams, and most importantly, of following through with commitments. She got into action immediately on arriving in her new home, found a job she liked, and began to connect with women in the community. Tina had always been passionate about health and fitness. She was one of the individuals in her Women Connected group who always worked out, paid attention to her diet, and loved to camp with friends. In Sitka she quickly began taking long hikes, not letting bad weather stand in her way. She has hiked in gale-force winds, deep snow, and horizontal torrents of rain.

As difficult as this physical activity sounds, the emotional challenges were tougher for Tina to overcome in Sitka. There were bumps along the way, but without family and friends close by, Keith and Tina discovered they were a very successful team. With her husband's love and support, Tina tackled the challenges involved in moving to a new state, and within a short time she began to feel that Sitka was her home. After four years they had their first child, a little girl named Carly.

During her last Women Connected session, each group member took time to acknowledge Tina, affirming her accomplishments and the difference she had made in each of their lives. Tears flowed freely; it was hard to imagine the group without her. As hard as it was to say good-bye to Tina, we knew in our hearts that she would be successful wherever she went—she had connected deeply with herself in ways that would support her for a lifetime. It was important that we had the opportunity to share this with her. And it was equally important that she have the opportunity to receive such affirming acknowledgments.

The Big Picture: Celebrating Us!

Suggested Time Frames	Activity	Purpose	Materials | Set-up
:05	Opening	Welcome; transition into Women Connected; become present	• Handout 11.1 "Stars"
:35	Check-In	Update, reconnect, report	• Candle for each woman • My Purpose statement • Completed Session Accelerator 11.1 20 Dreams in Motion list
:45	Session: Celebrating Us!	Share acknowledgments of accomplishments, changes, and break-throughs achieved during Women Connected	• Completed Session Accelerator 11.1 Women Connected Acknowledgments
:55	Pot Luck	Celebration of Women Connected	• Food and beverages
:10	Closing Circle	Complete the session and acknowledge experiences with Women Connected	• Standing circle • Extinguish candle

What Happens During the "Celebrating Us!" Session

0:00 WELCOME (5 MINUTES)

Prior to starting the group, place a candle for each woman near the location where the group will be gathered. Each woman will light a candle at the completion of her Check-In.

Group Guide welcomes the group to her home and this session.

Let's begin by taking three to four deep breaths. As you inhale, breathe deeply into all the possibilities waiting to be discovered. As you exhale, sink deeply into your authentic self and relax into a state of openness and connection to self, and be present to everything that you've achieved during the last 10 sessions in Women Connected.

Group Guide reads poem, "Stars."

HANDOUT 11.1: "STARS"

After the poem is read say:

Silently affirm to yourself the intention you're holding for this session. How will you show up for today's session, what will you contribute, and how will you demonstrate your support to the group?

Allow one minute of quiet reflection and then proceed to Check-In.

0:05 CHECK-IN (35 MINUTES)

Group Guide says:

Let's begin our Check-In.

Each person has four to five minutes to share her thoughts on the following topics:

☐ Begin by stating your purpose

☐ Describe the current status of your 20 Dreams in Motion

☐ What are you currently celebrating in your life?

Who would like to begin?

Remember that the Group Guide will model the time frame for Check-In. Tell the group that you'll be using the digital timer, and that when the four minutes are up, the next person to her right checks in. Be sure to stay within the four- to five-minute time frame.

What You'll Need

- Candle for each woman
- Digital timer
- Camera for group photo
- Handout 11.1 "Stars"
- Session Accelerator 11.1 20 Dreams in Motion
- Session Accelerator 11.1 Women Connected Acknowledgments
- A place to keep Acknowledgments
- Poster board, 4x16 inch ribbon, or a handmade Acknowledgments Book
- Tape recorder for Acknowledgment activity
- Food and beverages for celebration potluck

Session Accelerator and handouts are provided as downloadable files at www.WomenConnected.com

As each individual completes her Check-In, she lights a candle and states her intention for the session.

After Check-In is completed, proceed to the next activity.

0:40 INTRODUCTION TO CELEBRATING US! (5 MINUTES)

This is our final scheduled session of Women Connected. There is much to celebrate. We have accomplished amazing things together during our 11 sessions. Most important, we have discovered the power of connecting with one another through intentional conversations. We've worked through our resistance, supported one another in our goals, and listened deeply to what matters most. The focus of our session today will be to acknowledge one another for personal contributions that made a difference.

0:45 CELEBRATING US!
ACKNOWLEDGMENTS (40 MINUTES)

Each one of us will have the opportunity to be in the Seat of Honor. *(Indicate location of Seat of Honor.)* When you sit in this special place, each group member will share her acknowledgments with you. But before hearing from others, the person in the Seat of Honor will begin the process by sharing the answer to the following question:

☐ What do I appreciate about my life and myself?

After everyone has taken her turn, we'll exchange our written acknowledgments with one another.

After each woman in the Seat of Honor has shared her answer to the question, the group members take turns offering their acknowledgments to her. When these have been heard, the next woman in the circle moves to The Seat of Honor. This process continues until everyone has had an opportunity to hear acknowledgments from the group. Afterward, invite everyone to exchange their written acknowledgments with each other. You can put acknowledgments you receive in your personal journal, on a poster board, or attach them to a 4 x 16 inch ribbon. Some groups have created a small book filled with these acknowledgments. Be creative. The important thing is to keep your acknowledgments in a special place. On those days when you forget how great you are, bring out your Women Connected acknowledgments, read them, and let the appreciation of your friends wash over you as you remember who you are and what you contribute in your world.

Who would like to begin?

Remember: Don't rush this process. Take your time; really honor and celebrate each individual. When you have finished with each person, applaud her accomplishments and fully celebrate what they have meant to you during Women Connected.

1:25 CELEBRATION MEAL (55 MINUTES)

This is a time for fun, laughter, and eating and drinking together.

Here are a few suggestions of topics for conversation during the meal:

☐ My most memorable moment since we've been meeting.
☐ What's next? How do we want to continue Women Connected? It could be that we take a break, invite new women

into our group, and keep going as we have, or split up and start several new Women Connected groups.

When the Celebrating Us! meal is complete and the conversations regarding the group's future have been discussed, proceed to the Closing Circle.

2:20 CLOSING CIRCLE (10 MINUTES)

As we come together in this circle of Women Connected, we stand as wise and powerful women who together have accomplished more than we ever thought possible. Dreams have come true and friendships have deepened. At this special time and place, we'll each take a moment and share a brief thought or feeling about our celebration today.

Rotating around the Circle, each woman shares her feelings or thoughts. After everyone has shared in Closing Circle, say:
This session is complete. Please extinguish your candle until we connect again.

Take a group photo after Closing Circle.

Afterthoughts:
A Few Words from Kate

Kate has a big wide smile that reaches out and gently touches the people she meets. She's all about connections. In her 27 years, she's experienced a lifetime of joy, sorrow, and heartache. You'd never know it, though—her sense of humor is infectious. She tells me she wakes up each morning, centers herself, and finds her smile before starting her day. As difficult as it is for her to sit and be quiet during this morning ritual, Kate has learned that the payoff is worth the momentary discomfort. A firm believer in the value of personal growth, she has taken numerous workshops and is interested in alternative medicine. Kate works in a family business, and describes herself as being very close to her family. She thinks of herself as a writer and an artist who just happens to make her living in other ways. She dreams of creating an arts and wellness center for women and children. Kate's center will be a place where you can learn more about yourself, share stories with others, be creative, and explore the connection of mind, body, and spirit.

This is what Kate had to say about her experience during Celebrating Us! "What an incredible opportunity it has been to be provided a safe and nurturing forum to give heartfelt and thoughtful appreciations to others, and to receive such a beautiful gift in return. I was overcome with tears of joy at the bravery and inspiration it took to share our thoughts and feelings. This experience reminded me of what a valuable tool it is to have verbal and written testimonies to our own self-worth. It is not easy to sit and receive such gifts, but as I looked around the room that evening, I was comforted knowing that the truth was being spoken by women I honored and respected.

"I find the impact of this event has me physically walking taller, holding my head higher, and smiling a lot wider, knowing I am held in high regard by powerful, confident women. What I found most amazing was the similar sentiments that we each shared about one another; almost identical words and phrases were used to describe each woman in the room. Regardless of our differences in lifestyle, behavior, or beliefs, we all found that we embody a very similar essence. We are each filled with the desire to lead purposeful lives, where we feel our most empowered. We may have different paths toward this goal, but the encouragement we shared and received from one another is proving to be a powerful tool of affirmation on our journey.

"When I reflect on the messages I received, I am able to reaffirm my influence and impact in this world. I know that others see me as I am learning to see myself: as a woman of confidence, compassion, and respect. The validation I received from this experience inspires me to break down the negative self-talk that I tend to harbor within, and continually strive toward my higher purposes in life."

Last Thoughts

During the last nine months—yes, exactly the amount of time it takes to give birth—I've been writing, reflecting, and rewriting to be certain I had included all that was needed to complete this foundational Women Connected guide. And now, as the book draws to its conclusion, I'm imagining all the different women's groups that will make use of this first book in the Women Connected series. I can see Women Connected for Single Parents, for Grandmothers, for Mothers and Daughters, for Women in Transition, for Twenty-Somethings, for Young Mothers—each group of women with their own unique blend of life experience, putting their dreams into motion. It's a thrilling vision!

Throughout the last three decades as I've facilitated and been a member of women's support groups, again and again I have come to the same conclusion: When women come together in support of one another, when intentional conversations take place in which stories and dreams are shared, literally *anything* is possible, and magic occurs.

Remember the magic you've shared together, the accomplishments of your coaching group, the laughter and the tears. Together you've created memories that will last a lifetime, and as you go forward, new memories will emerge. Take your connectedness out into the world; share yourself with others who have lost touch with the magic of connection. If each one of us resolved to do this, our world might begin to heal through the compassion, love, and strength of women connecting.

Many years ago a friend of mine gave me a sparkling magic wand that makes a lovely sound resembling wind chimes. Over the years I have playfully used my magic wand as a fairy godmother might, to bestow blessings on the dreams of my clients. I encourage you to find your own magic wand to symbolize all that you've created in your life and all that you'll continue to create as you go forward into the future.

Thank you for choosing Women Connected to guide and coach your group. I wish you a lifetime of joy, love, and deepening connections.

Handout 11.1

STARS

by Margaret Wheatley
Turning to One Another

In places where air still offers clarity,
stars sing a siren song from space
in the bright night.

Lying on soft earth,
carried into sky by longing,
humans respond to stars
with questions. Why is the Universe
so vast? Why are we so small?

Call and response through the night.

My whole life I have sent
these questions into space. And
listened for response.

Then sky wakens and star song fades.
Humans forget mystery and get on
with living.
But the stars, the stars
keep calling. No response.

Why is it that we call to
stars with science and insignificance?

On the next bright night,
find the clear air and ask again.
Humans, ask again. Who are we?
What is our place in mystery?

Perhaps you will hear what I
have heard, a song of inner
radiance.

For the stars
the stars are calling

saying we must
turn to one another
turn to one another and see
finally see
the stars everywhere.

Note: In a clear night sky, for every star we see, there are 50 million more behind it.

Resources

Group Guide Checklist
Everything You Need to Know and More!

Just like an airline pilot who has a checklist before taking off, now so do you! If you follow this checklist, you will be assured of hosting a wonderful session.

PREPARATION

☐ Read through the directions for the session several times until you're comfortable with your role in leading the group.

☐ Select a special poem or brief story to share with group.

☐ Make copies of the handouts for each group member.

☐ Purchase a candle for each woman. It's okay to use tea lights, the candles don't need to be expensive.

☐ Prepare snacks and beverages for the end of the session.

PLACE

☐ Select a place in your home that is comfortable, uncluttered, and can comfortably seat the group.

☐ If possible, arrange the chairs and couches in a circle, so all women will be facing one another.

☐ Place a small table in the middle of the circle or nearby to hold the candles.

SELF CARE

☐ Take five or ten minutes before the women arrive to relax, take some deep breaths, and center yourself.

☐ Set your intention for the session.

SETTING THE MOOD

☐ Select a piece of music that will provide a soothing transition from the outside world to the Women Connected session.

☐ Start the music before the first woman arrives.

☐ When the group starts, turn off the music.

WELCOMING GROUP MEMBERS

☐ Personally greet each woman as she arrives.

☐ Set the pace by modeling a non-rushed type of greeting.

TIMEKEEPER

☐ You are in charge of keeping things moving during the session.

☐ Set a timer before the women arrive to alert you to the beginning of the session.

☐ When the timer goes off, invite the women into the circle to start the session.

☐ Ask for the group's support in keeping things moving according to the suggested time frame.

☐ If a segment of the session seems to be taking extra time, ask the group if they want to stay late or stop and go to the next activity.

ONE MORE THING

☐ Remember, you are the facilitator of this session.

☐ Make certain that everyone has an opportunity to be heard.

☐ Participate in all activities and group discussions.

☐ Even if you're tempted, don't dominate the group!

Things That Might Go Wrong— Troubleshooting Tips for Women Connected

Whatever our patterns of communication are, they will become evident in the Women Connected group. We're often unconscious of the pattern until someone points it out. Only when it becomes obvious to us can we choose to communicate differently. Everyone has blind spots. It's only when someone cares enough to shed light on those blind spots that change can take place. Below you'll find some common unproductive communication patterns. My wish is that this Troubleshooting guide supports you in creating a powerful Women Connected group.

INTERRUPTING THE SPEAKER

As a general rule, most of the interruptions that occur during a group are unconscious. I've learned that naming the issue brings it into everyone's awareness, and this significantly minimizes interruptions. You might say, "I've been noticing that some of us often interrupt with questions, advice, or how my life is similar or different from yours. I'd like us to recommit as a group to take personal responsibility to remain alert to communication patterns that interfere with individual sharing."

ADVICE-GIVING

This pattern can be extremely disruptive, due to the fact that advice is often unsolicited. Offering advice presupposes that the giver knows more about the situation and has more wisdom than the person sharing. From time to time we all like to receive advice to expand our thinking and broaden our choices. When someone asks for advice, it's often helpful to ask questions that elicit the group member's own existing wisdom on the topic. If a group member feels really stuck, there's a great Women Connected process for identifying possible solutions: the Wisdom Blast. (Read about the Wisdom Blast in "Getting Started" at the front of this book.)

STARTING THE SESSIONS LATE

Ultimately it is the Group Guide who ensures that each Women Connected session starts and ends promptly. If you notice it's time to start or end, give the group a gentle nudge by saying something like, "I'm noticing it's time to begin. Let's get started." Or, "Our time today has gone by fast and it's almost time to begin our Closing Circle." It helps to have a ritual for the beginning and end of each session, for example, ringing a small bell to signify the beginning, or setting a digital timer before the group arrives to ensure a timely start to the session. Rituals become group norms over time and are difficult to ignore—even when the most fascinating social conversations are taking place. Rather than delay starting while the group waits for a late arrival, I suggest starting the Women Connected session on time so the one who is late experiences the natural consequence of missing some of the Check-In time. Setting group standards and adhering to your Connecting Principles is critical to maintaining a successful experience for everyone.

FEELING RUSHED AND RUNNING OUT OF TIME

Of all the things that can go wrong, this is the one complaint I hear most often from Women Connected groups. When an important conversation takes place, it's natural to want to continue and delay moving on to the next activity. When this happens, however, the time is shortened for whatever follows. Soon you find yourselves rushing though the remaining activities in order to end the session on time. If this happens more than once, it's time to evaluate what the group wants to do. One option is to lengthen the sessions to accommodate the extra time needed to complete the activities. Another option is to take two sessions to complete each topic. In this case you would follow each of the recurring

Women Connected elements (Check-In, Capturing What Matters Most to Me, My Commitments, Closing Circle, etc.) and simply divide each topic's activities into two sessions. If these two options don't work, you'll need to be more rigorous with the recommended starting and stopping times. Trust me, it can be done!

NOT COMPLETING THE SESSION ACCELERATOR

People have busy schedules and occasionally completing the Session Accelerator may not make it onto someone's to-do list. Even with the best intentions, sometimes we forget or fall behind with our life choices. If a person habitually does not complete her Session Accelerator, however, the time has come to address the issue within the group. Her inaction affects the entire group, so it makes sense to discuss the Connecting Principles. Such a discussion can be set up as a review of the Principles, in which all group members have the opportunity to recommit to them or change them. Exploring what gets in the way of completing the Session Accelerators can open up the topic of other areas of one's life that may be incomplete. Remember, this is not a group that judges people for their choices, but it is important to address the impact of the choice.

CHRONIC ABSENCES AND LATE ARRIVALS

If one or more women are missing sessions on a regular basis, it's time for a group discussion. Typically, if someone misses sessions regularly, something is up—and it needs to be discussed. Possible areas of exploration might include the level of commitment to Women Connected, changes in life priorities, resistance or resentment related to group practices, or a breakdown in group trust and integrity. During this conversation it is crucial to be as honest as possible. Part of the discussion will be a description of the specific behavior and its impact on the group's success. Then you will move on to generating ideas to remedy the situation. A Wisdom Blast can be used to explore solutions to this issue. Again, this is not about finding fault or placing blame. The situation is an opportunity to increase trust and commitment to the group's success.

SIDE TALKING

It's quite distracting when someone speaks to her neighbor while another person is addressing the group during an activity. When side talking occurs, you can be sure that deep listening is not happening. It's impossible to give full attention to one person while carrying on a conversation with someone else. So what can be done? When I'm addressing the group and some-one else begins talking at the same time, I often simply stop mid-sentence. This draws attention to the side talking, and it usually stops abruptly. Before side talking ever occurs, it's important to discuss it with the group so you can agree in advance how to handle it. This might be part of defining your Connecting Principles. When things get off track, what will you do? Since it takes two women to be engaged in side talk, the recipient of the comment might choose not to respond. For some people, side talking is simply part of the way they connect with others. They may be blind to this pattern and, in the Women Connected group, it can be very disruptive. Pointing it out can be a valuable service.

GOSSIPING OUTSIDE THE SESSION

As tempting as it might be to gossip, don't do it under any circumstances. If you are bothered by something or someone in the group, commit to bringing the issue forward. Nothing undermines the trust in a group quicker than finding out that confidentiality or trust has been broken. In many cases, the way to address this issue is similar to side talking. If someone begins to talk about another person outside of the group, and you are the recipient of this gossip, state your commitment to saying what needs to be said in the group and not to engage in be said in the group and not to engage in gossip. Of course it is perfectly okay to discuss your own issues, and this is encouraged, especially with your Growth Buddy.

GROWTH BUDDIES NOT CONNECTING BETWEEN SESSIONS

The Growth Buddy system of support and accountability is a unique and important feature of Women Connected. It has a proven track record of working to keep you focused on creating the life of your dreams. Over the course of 11 sessions, you'll be connecting with each woman as a Growth Buddy. In this way you'll develop a deeper relationship with everyone in the group. It is important to be specific about when you'll connect, how you'll contact each other (e-mail, telephone, in person), and who will initiate the contact. Backup plans are essential, because occasionally it will be necessary to reschedule. If you tend to these guidelines, you'll have a successful Growth Buddy experience. See also the Growth Buddies guidelines in the Resources section.

CHECK-IN TAKING LONGER THAN NECESSARY

It feels good to connect, especially if you haven't seen some of the group members for a few weeks. The Group Guide is in charge of keeping the Check-In on sched-

ule. Setting a digital timer before each person begins her Check-In will assist in keeping the updates brief and to the point. If extra-long Check-Ins are an ongoing group problem, you might use a Wisdom Blast to come up with various solutions.

GROUP MEMBER POSITIONING HERSELF AS AN EXPERT

We can readily accept someone stepping forward as knowledgeable on a specific topic. However, if the same woman acts like an expert in just about everything, this can be a problem for the group. When this happens advice flows freely, and that's not always helpful. Please take a moment and re-read the section on Advice Giving.

GROUP MEMBER USING WOMEN CONNECTED IN PLACE OF A THERAPIST

One group member may frequently bring up past events, and may seem to have difficulty either staying in the present or planning for the future. Through her sharing, it becomes clear that she has unresolved issues that need therapeutic help. Examples of such issues are addictions, physical or emotional abuse, or deep-seated unresolved anger. Beware of this behavior monopolizing group time. Women Connected is designed to support you in moving toward your future, not to settle unresolved issues from the past. In such situations, I suggest a one-on-one conversation with the individual. Who initiates this conversation? If you are concerned about it, you might be the right person to bring it up. Share your concern privately, stating that this Women Connected group is not equipped to handle these particular issues. You might recommend a therapist that you know or assist her in finding a professional trained in dealing with the issues of concern to her.

SPECIAL HELP FOR DIFFICULT ISSUES

If your Women Connected group encounters a problem not addressed here, you may e-mail your question to info@Women Connected.com to request suggestions on how to address your issue.

Growth Buddy—A Support System

Early on, when I first started the Women Connected group process, I discovered two drawbacks inherent in meeting only once a month. The first problem showed up when one of the members missed a session. This meant she was disconnected from the group for two months! Although I spoke with her a few times to update her about what had happened in the session she missed, we had no face-to-face contact with her during those two months. Over the course of the second month, she decided to withdraw. The group was still at the early stage of formation, and her level of connection and commitment to the other members was not yet strong.

Although each group decides how often to meet, it works well (at least for the first three sessions) to meet every two weeks. This builds a solid foundation of connection between group members.

The second problem was the frequent calls I was receiving between sessions. At first, fielding questions seemed to be my job as the coach/facilitator. Yet one of the goals I had set for the coaching groups was for members to begin coaching each other and connecting in meaningful ways between sessions. Thus the Growth Buddies system was born.

I envisioned Growth Buddies as a positive first step for the women to begin connecting at deeper levels, forming friendships, and participating in peer coaching. I also anticipated that the system would help solidify individual commitments to the long-term success of the group. The members soon discovered what worked, where challenges showed up, and what kinds of possibilities opened up as they connected and supported each other in reaching their goals.

One of the great benefits is that Growth Buddies are available to each other on a timely basis. They can connect as often as they choose to connect between the sessions. This support system frees up the coach/facilitator and truly empowers the group to take charge of their own lives. As our group began using this system, the women became increasingly independent between sessions and trusted their inner wisdom more often as they moved forward in their lives.

Think about the coaches or teachers who have played a positive role in your life. What made them special? How did they make a difference for you? How would your life be different if you hadn't connected with them? We remember people who open up new vistas of knowledge, challenge our beliefs, unsettle our minds, and believe in us when we're unable or unwilling to believe in ourselves. Growth Buddies provide a similar experience that makes a big difference in the lives of the Women Connected coaching group members. This buddy system provides a place outside the group to celebrate each other's accomplishments, listen to each other's dreams, and help each other stay focused on personal goals. The learning, discovery, and new insight that emerge in each group session are carried forward and continue to expand and develop with gentle nudging from the Growth Buddy. And it's fun!

GROWTH BUDDY STORIES

During Check-In each woman takes a couple of minutes to bring the group up to date on what's going on in her life, and describes what she experienced with her Growth Buddy between sessions. This doesn't need to take very long—just describing the highlights will help to connect the group before moving forward with the new topic or activity. Sometimes the Growth Buddy experiences are surprisingly magical and inspiring. As each new experience is shared, members strengthen their commitment to the ongoing process of Women Connected.

One evening Sue described what it was like to have Mary as her Growth Buddy. The previous session they had randomly ended up with each other, and they were working on two very different issues for which they needed support. Mary had always been quite thin and has had great difficulty keeping weight on for any length of time. She expressed a desire to gain weight so she could feel more comfortable with her body. In that particular session, Sue had decided to address the opposite issue. She had spent most of her life struggling with being overweight, with only short-term success. Nothing seemed to work; she had grown tired of all the diets and broken promises to herself over the years. Together Mary and Sue decided to attend a 40-30-30 seminar—a nutritional course that educates individuals about healthy food choices. After attending three classes together, they were both firmly committed to achieving their goals—Mary to gaining weight and Sue to losing weight and keeping it off. Together they were accomplishing what they hadn't been able to do alone—two women connected!

During Check-In one evening, a woman shared quite a different experience with her Growth Buddy. Kate had wanted to finish an interior painting and wallpapering project in her home. Several months had gone by and she seemed unable to move forward. In her own words, she was hopelessly stuck. Her Growth Buddy of the month, Nancy, went along with her to shop for wallpaper. They had a great time together finding just the right wallpaper for Kate's home. Later they spent a Sunday afternoon wallpapering Kate's kitchen, and celebrated their accomplishment by sharing a pizza. This may sound like a small thing—not at all life changing or earth shattering—but for Kate it made a real difference. By giving Kate a gentle nudge, Nancy helped her to move forward in completing a project that had become an obstacle in her life, and they formed a great bond in the process!

What obstacles do you face? There are so many things we dream of doing that don't seem to get done. While these untended wishes may seem like no more than a nuisance right now, in the long run putting off our dreams and pet projects can drain our energy and health. It's a wonderful gift to have a Growth Buddy to support us in clearing up whatever is incomplete in our lives, as we move forward in the pursuit of our dreams.

Growth Buddy Guidelines— Giving and Receiving Support

Identify what you want to accomplish.

- ☐ What are the measurable results you want?
- ☐ How will you know them when you see them?
- ☐ What is an acceptable time frame for achieving them?
- ☐ What is the essence of what you want?
- ☐ What feeling will your results provide you?
- ☐ How will these results change your life?
- ☐ What will your relationships with others and yourself look like?
- ☐ What will be the quality and direction of your life?

Design action steps that support your success.

- ☐ Commit to achieving your results.
- ☐ Make a symbol for it. A picture, a poem on the refrigerator, etc.
- ☐ Make the commitment feel real; create rituals.
- ☐ Mark off the steps or calendar days until you achieve it.
- ☐ Celebrate your successes along the way.

Identify your reward for keeping your commitment.

- ☐ What will it look like?

- ☐ How will it feel?

Some examples:

- ☐ Others will trust and respect me more.
- ☐ I'll trust and respect myself more.
- ☐ I'll feel more self-confidence and self-love.

Determine the consequence of breaking your commitment.

- ☐ What will that look like?
- ☐ How will it feel?

Some examples:

- ☐ It will erode others' trust and respect for me.
- ☐ It will erode my trust and respect for myself.
- ☐ It will lower my self-confidence and self-love.

Schedule a meeting with your Growth Buddy.

- ☐ Who will call whom?
- ☐ When?
- ☐ How often?
- ☐ How long?

Ask your Growth Buddy for support.

- ☐ Tell your Growth Buddy the results you want, and your commitment to yourself.
- ☐ Share how important this is to you.
- ☐ Get her agreement to support you.

Describe what support means to you.

- ☐ How much feedback would you like?
- ☐ What tone of voice does and doesn't work?
- ☐ What works for you and what doesn't?

Growth Buddies in Action

- ☐ Tell the truth; stick to the issue in the here-and-now.
- ☐ Be 100 percent accountable.
- ☐ Know that if you don't like it, you can change it!
- ☐ There is an opportunity to learn and choose again.
- ☐ Acknowledge even small increments of success.
- ☐ Consistently identify and let go of any attitudes, behaviors, and feelings that don't support your goals and dreams.

Believing in yourself, accomplishing your goals.

- ☐ Hold a vision of yourself keeping your agreement.
- ☐ Don't give up on yourself—even if you need to change your planned results.
- ☐ Your Growth Buddy holds the vision of you keeping agreements and commitments. No matter what results are appearing temporarily, she will not give up on you.
- ☐ No matter what obstacles or boulders show up, she sees you having exactly what you want.
- ☐ "You want it? You can have it. Don't let go of your visions and dreams."

What happens when you keep your commitments?

- ☐ Acknowledge even small successes.

     "Great. You've completed the first step. You're on your way!"

- ☐ Express your supportive vision.

     "I see you as a winner."

     "I see you keeping your agreement."

What happens when you don't keep your commitments?
- ☐ Determine whether commitment is still current.
    "Do you still want to achieve this goal?"

Lapses are for learning; they are not failures. Hold your vision of success. "I will hold my vision of you succeeding, whether or not you keep it. You are worth all the effort we are putting into this. You deserve success!"

Identify the reasons or excuses for breaking your commitments.
- ☐ Acknowledge the ineffectiveness of the excuses or reasons.
- ☐ No blame; no guilt; new learning, insights, and awareness are available.
- ☐ Recommit.

Mistakes and lapses provide valuable information about:
- ☐ What we don't want anymore.
- ☐ What we do want.
- ☐ Our motivation to go the final stretch.

We only fail if we choose to give up, and even that is only temporary. Hold your vision of keeping the agreement . . . no matter how long it takes.

Celebrate Success!
- ☐ Celebrate with your Growth Buddy.
- ☐ Thank and reward your Growth Buddy in meaningful ways.
- ☐ Acknowledge yourself for your success.
- ☐ Note what you learned along the way.
- ☐ Enjoy your success; you deserve to see your dreams come true!

en Growth Buddies Meet—A Suggested Structure

1. Check-In and social time
   (catch up on relationships/work/play/stressors)

2. Ask, "How's your _____ going?"
   (check in on goals, action plans, commitments)

3. Generate new possibilities

4. Renew commitments

5. Clear up any obstacles

6. Ask for the help you need before the next session

7. Celebrate together

8. Set up the next time to connect

9. Good-byes!

Taking a Deeper Look

Here is a list of resources for those who desire to expand their knowledge about the Women Connected session topics.

Chapter 1 Evening of Exploration

Brown, Juanita. *The World Cafe: Shaping Our Futures Through Conversations That Matter.* San Francisco: Berrett-Koehler Publishers, 2005.

Dreamer, Oriah Mountain. *The Invitation.* San Francisco: HarperSanFrancisco, 1999.

Satir, Virginia. *Making Contact.* Berkeley, California: Celestial Arts, 1976.

Wheatley, Margaret J. *Turning to One Another: Simple Conversations to Restore Hope to the Future.* San Francisco: Berrett-Koehler Publishers, 2002.

Chapter 2 New Beginnings

Baldwin, Christina. *Calling the Circle: The First and Future Culture.* New York: Bantam Books, 1998.

Bolen, Jean Shinoda. *The Millionth Circle: How to Change Ourselves and the World.* Berkeley, California: Conari Press, 1999.

Carnes, Robin Deen, and Sally Crag. *Sacred Circles: A Guide to Creating Your Own Women's Spirituality Group.* San Francisco: HarperSanFrancisco, 1998.

Engel, Beverly. *Women Circling the Earth: A Guide to Fostering Community, Healing and Empowerment.* Deerfield Beach, Florida: Health Communications, 2000.

Garfield, Charles, Cindy Spring, and Sedonia Cahill. *Wisdom Circles: A Guide to Self-Discovery and Community Building in Small Groups.* New York: Hyperion, 1998.

Chapter 3 Seasons of My Life

Hudson, Frederic M., and Pamela D. McLean. *Life Launch: A Passionate Guide to the Rest of Your Life.* Santa Barbara, California: The Hudson Institute Press, 2001.

Heckler, Richard Strozzi. *The Anatomy of Change: A Way to Move Through Life's Transitions.* Berkeley, California: North Atlantic Books, 1993.

Northrup, Christiane. *Women's Bodies, Women's Wisdom.* New York: Bantam, 1998.

Rosenberg, Marshall B. *Nonviolent Communication: A Language of Life.* Encinitas, California: Puddle Dancer Press, 2003.

ter 4 Calling on Purpose

ne, Carol. *Find Your Purpose, Change Your Life: Getting to the Heart of Your Life's Mission.* New York: Harper Collins, 2001.

Leider, Richard J. *The Power of Purpose: Creating Meaning in Your Life and Work.* San Francisco: Berrett-Koehler Publishers, 1997.

Levoy, Gregg. *Callings: Finding and Following an Authentic Life.* New York: Three Rivers Press, 1997.

Schuster, John P. *Answering Your Call: A Guide for Living Your Deepest Purpose.* San Francisco: Berrett-Koehler Publishers, 2003.

Chapter 5 Future Perfect

Grout, Pam. *Living Big: Embrace Your Passion and Leap Into an Extraordinary Life.* Berkeley, California: Conari Press, 2001.

Sher, Barbara, and Barbara Smith. *I Could Do Anything if I Only Knew What It Was: How to Discover What You Really Want and How to Get It.* New York: Dell Publishing, 1994.

Ryan, M.J., editor. *The Fabric of the Future: Women Visionaries Illuminate the Path to Tomorrow.* Berkeley, California: Conari Press, 1998.

Zander, Rosamund Stone, and Benjamin Zander. *The Art of Possibility: Transforming Professional and Personal Life.* Boston: Harvard Business School Press, 2000.

Chapter 6 Dreams in Motion

Richardson, Cheryl. *Take Time for Your Life.* New York: Broadway Books, 1999.

Sher, Barbara. *Live the Life You Love.* New York: Dell Publishing, 1996.

Wieder, Marcia. *Making Your Dreams Come True.* New York: Harmony Books, 1999.

Chapter 7 The Mythology of Me

Brehony, Kathleen A. *Awakening at Midlife: A Guide to Reviving Your Spirit, Recreating Your Life, and Returning to Your Truest Self.* New York: Riverhead Books, 1997.

Markova, Dawna. *I Will Not Die an Unlived Life: Reclaiming Purpose and Passion.* Boston: Red Wheel/Weiser, LLC, 2000.

Williamson, Marianne. *The Gift of Change: Spiritual Guidance for a Radically New Life.* San Francisco: HarperSanFrancisco, 2004.

Chapter 8 The Brand of Me

Cameron, Julia. *The Artist's Way.* New York: G.P. Putnam's Sons, 1992.

Sark. *Succulent Wild Woman: Dancing with Your Wonder-Full Self!* New York: Fireside, 1997.

Smith, Keri. *Living Out Loud: Activities to Fuel a Creative Life.* San Francisco: Chronicle Books, 2003.

Chapter 9 Breaking Through Obstacles

Jeffers, Susan. *Feel the Fear and Beyond.* New York: Ballantine Books, 1998.

Maurer, Rick. *Beyond the Wall of Resistance.* Austin, Texas: Bard Press, 1996.

Smith, David Miln, and Sandra Leicester. *Hug the Monster: How to Embrace Your Fears and Live Your Dreams.* Kansas City, Missouri: Andrews and McMeel, 1996.

Chapter 10 Courageous Conversations

Patterson, Kerry, Joseph Grenny, Ron McMillan, Al Switzler and Stephen R. Covey. *Crucial Conversations: Tools for Talking When Stakes are High.* New York: McGraw-Hill, 2002.

Scott, Susan. *Fierce Conversations: Achieving Success at Work and in Life, One Conversation at a Time.* New York: Berkley Publishing Group, 2004.

Stone, Douglas, Bruce Patton, and Sheila Heen. *Difficult Conversations: How to Discuss What Matters Most.* New York: Penguin Books, 2000.

Chapter 11 Celebrating Us!

Adams, Caroline Joy. *A Woman of Wisdom: Honoring and Celebrating Who You Are.* Berkeley, California: Celestial Arts, 1999.

Louden, Jennifer. *The Woman's Retreat Book: A Guide to Restoring, Rediscovering, and Reawakening Your True Self.* San Francisco: HarperSanFrancisco, 1997.

Northrup, Christiane. *Mother-Daughter Wisdom: Creating a Legacy of Physical and Emotional Health.* New York: Bantam, 2005.

ry

...st of poetry books is provided to assist the Group Guide in her selection of poems for each session.

Angelou, Maya. *Phenomenal Woman: Four Poems Celebrating Women.* New York: Random House, 1995.

Braybrooke, Marcus, Editor. *The Bridge of Stars: 365 Prayers, Blessings, and Meditations from Around the World.* London: Thorsons, 2001.

Brussat, Frederic and Mary Ann. *Spiritual Rx: Prescriptions for Living a Meaningful Life.* New York: Hyperion, 2000.

Donnelly, Margarita, Beverly McFarland, and Micki Reaman, editors. *A Fierce Brightness: Twenty-five Years of Women's Poetry.* Corvallis, Oregon: Calyx Books, 2002.

Hirschfield, Jane, editor. *Women in Praise of the Sacred: 43 Centuries of Spiritual Poetry by Women.* New York: HarperCollins, 1993.
————*The Lives of the Heart: Poems.* New York: Harper Perennial, 1997.

Mulford, Wendy, editor. *Love Poems by Women: An Anthology of Poetry from Around the World and Through the Ages.* New York: Ballantine Books, 1991.

Oliver, Mary. *Blue Iris: Poems and Essays.* Boston: Beacon Press, 2004.
————*New and Selected Poems: Volume One.* Boston: Beacon Press, 2004.
————*New and Selected Poems: Volume Two.* Boston: Beacon Press, 2005.

For even more resources, please visit **www.WomenConnected.com**.

Web Sites

The web sites of the organizations listed here provide a variety of ways to connect with service organizations and community-building programs that your Women Connected group may want to work with as a team, or consider individually. The need to contribute our gifts and talents, our love and help, often comes up during the Calling on Purpose or Dreams in Motion sessions. Your group might also wish to offer their time and support to one of these groups as part of Celebrating Us!

Childrenshungerfund.org
Since 1991, the Children's Hunger Fund has transformed children's lives from hunger to hope. Thousands of compassionate families fill Food Paks, and then deliver the food directly into the homes of needy families. Volunteers also help wrap the thousands of toys given to children during the holiday season.

Heifer.org
Heifer Project International is a nonprofit organization that helps hungry people feed themselves, earn income, and care for the environment. Long term solutions emphasizing community involvement distinguish their work from other global relief organizations.

Millionthcircle.org
An extraordinary site with a huge vision—to change the world into a place of peace and worldwide healing by supporting and empowering women's circles.

Projectlinus.org
Project Linus is a 100% volunteer non-profit organization whose mission is to provide a sense of security, warmth and comfort to children who are seriously ill or traumatized by events in their lives. The children receive new, handmade blankets and afghans, lovingly created by volunteer "blanketeers." This would be a fun project for your Women Connected group!

Womenforwomen.org
Women for Women International helps women in war-torn regions rebuild their lives by providing financial aid, emotional support, job skills training, and access to business skills, capital and markets. By choosing to become a sponsor, your Women Connected group provides an impoverished woman the hope she needs to rebuild her life after war. Your letters will be an emotional lifeline to a woman who may have lost everything.

For even more resources, please visit **www.WomenConnected.com.**

owledgments

.... .leeply indebted to many people for their invaluable contributions to this book.

First of all, I'd like to thank all the women who chose Women Connected as a vehicle to connect, learn, and grow. I'm honored to know you and humbled by your courage, strength, and willingness to embrace change. Without your encouragement to make this work available on a larger scale, this book would not exist.

My current Wisdom Circle, which has been together for nine wondrous years, has enriched my life beyond measure. Linda Dunn, Carol Henry, Debbie Daniels, Victoria Castle, Cheryl Waale, Anne Fontaine, Peggy McKasy, and Stella Rabaut are the women I want to grow old with on this journey of life.

And I want to express my heartfelt gratitude to all the women who belonged to my personal Circles over the last 30 years, and who have played a significant role in me becoming who I am today—especially Susan Lynch, Diann Lavik, and Cheryl Esposito.

In the early stages of writing this book, three women—Marley Rynd, Mavis Tsai and Debbie Daniels—graciously volunteered to facilitate women's groups using my designs. Their thoughtful feedback and valuable suggestions helped me expand and deepen my original designs into a more user-friendly format.

Each story in the book is about a real woman, each of whom generously allowed me to tell their story, and share their life-changing experiences with Women Connected groups. A big thank you to Debbie, Darlene, Freddie, Sonia, Deanna, Lori, Gretchen, Linda, Jennifer, Tiffany, Tina, and Kate.

To my teachers, who have profoundly influenced my thinking, touched my heart, and often saw in and for me possibilities that I wasn't able to see for myself: Joan Kennedy, Gerry Rose, Audrey Williams, Will Schutz, Frederic Hudson, Pamela McLean, and Richard Strozzi Heckler.

To my dear friend Faith Wilder who has become part of our family: thank you for the priceless gift of time spent in proofing the book.

I am indebted to my editor, Ceci Miller, for being a paragon of patience and mentoring me through each stage of the book-writing process. This book is a reflection of her great wisdom, unwavering support, and belief in the importance of women supporting each other in their personal and professional lives.

And I want to thank Ceci's talented team—each of whom helped make this book a reality.

Shannon McCafferty, whose exceptional talent as a designer is evident in the book's innovative and gorgeous interior design, as well as in her brilliance in developing the cover concept.

Obadinah Heavner, a seasoned and gifted illustrator, who created a dazzling, eye-catching cover that captures the essence of Women Connected in the most magnificent ways.

Valerie Sensabaugh for her skillful copyediting and overall production expertise.

I am thankful for the early influence of my parents and all the lessons learned. To my father, Richard, for his unconditional love. To my grandparents for seeing me as a loving and capable woman. To my sister, Penny, for being a constant model of courage, optimism, and enthusiasm for life. To her husband, Bill, for being a wonderful dad, loving husband, and great friend, who made time in his busy schedule to proof my book. To my niece Tiffany for her sense of adventure and zest for life. To my niece Megan for reminding me of what matters most.

Words cannot express the depth of my love for our children, Keith and Deanna. I'm proud to be your mom, and I treasure our moments together, each experience creating another opportunity to create a family tradition! Thank you for choosing spouses that are a perfect fit for our family: Tina who has always been a second daughter to us, and Todd who has become our second son.

And I'm very grateful to our children for bringing new lives into our family, with the birth of our grandchildren, Oliver Joseph Wilday and Carly Jo Shuler. Our lives are blessed and enriched by their presence. Each day I am keenly aware of the preciousness of life and of our obligation as people to connect with those who matter most in our lives—and ultimately to remain connected to our dreams so that those who follow us know how to do the same.

My last acknowledgment is to the love of life, my husband and best friend, Blaine. He has been my resident editor and cheerleader, offering unconditional support, continual expressions of love, and neverending belief in me. His grounded presence held me steady each step of the way, and I am the luckiest woman in the world to have him forever by my side.

Index

Index of Handouts and Session Accelerators

Programs with Pam

WOMEN CONNECTED PROGRAMS, RETREATS,
AND KEYNOTE PRESENTATIONS

Please call 1-800-693-4919 or go to www.WomenConnected.com

1. Women Connected Group Launch
2. Truth or Consequences—Keeping Good Connections
3. Courageous Conversations for Women
4. Women Calling on Purpose
5. Making Dreams Come True with Women Connected
6. Celebrating Connection: A Women's Retreat

Pam Bartlett
c/o Glenmoore Press
P.O. Box 68
Greenbank, WA 98253
Phone: 1-800-693-4919
www.WomenConnected.com

Order Form

WOMEN CONNECTED

Pam Bartlett

Quantity	Title	Price US	Price Canada	Total
	Women Connected Pam Bartlett	$24.95	$29.95	
Shipping & Handling				$4.95 US
Sales Tax (WA state residents only, add 8.9%)				
Total Enclosed				

☐ Visa

☐ MasterCard

_____ _____ _____ _____   _____ / _____

Card Number   Expiration Date

Signature

☐ Check or money order enclosed
   Make Payable to: Glenmoore Press

Order by phone	Order by mail	Order online
1-800-693-4919	Glenmoore Press P.O. Box 68 Greenbank, WA. 98253	www.WomenConnected.com

Autographed copies and quantity discounts available at www.WomenConnected.com

Name

Address

City   State   Zip

Phone (   )   Fax (   )

For more information, e-mail info@WomenConnected.com. Thank you for your order!